Competing for Students, Money, and Reputation

MARKETING THE ACADEMY IN THE 21ST CENTURY

LARRY D. LAUER
TEXAS CHRISTIAN UNIVERSITY

ISBN 0-89964-371-X
Printed in the United States of America

The Council for Advancement and Support of Education is the largest international association of education institutions, serving more than 3,200 universities, colleges, schools, and related organizations in 45 countries. CASE is the leading resource for professional development, information, and standards in the fields of education fund raising, communications, and alumni relations.

Design: Design 291, www.design291.com
Editor: Theodore Fischer

COUNCIL FOR ADVANCEMENT
AND SUPPORT OF EDUCATION®

1307 New York Avenue NW
Suite 1000
Washington DC 20005-4701
www.case.org/books

TABLE OF CONTENTS

Preface

This book is the distillation of what has been learned over the last seven years as we at Texas Christian University have attempted to adapt the latest thinking about marketing to higher education. Visits to campuses large and small in the United States and abroad, countless appearances at conferences and workshops, and daily e-mail conversations with colleagues representing all type of institutions have been part of the research as well.

Actually, it all began with the collapse of the Southwest Athletic Conference and our concern about its impact on the TCU athletic program. The University of Texas, Texas A&M, Texas Tech, and Baylor announced that they were leaving the conference, and the press was reporting that the rest of us were "being left behind." Of course, our alumni and supporters everywhere were deeply concerned, to say the least. After over 100 years of athletics history and everyone being accustomed to a long and storied Division I tradition, TCU was without a conference and getting negative press every day.

Our response was to form a group of community leaders, the Committee of 100, with the simple objective of turning this potential negative into a positive. The Committee of 100 was formed under the chairmanship of John Roach, chairman of the TCU Board of Trustees and chairman and CEO of Tandy Corporation. The group hit the ground running to assess the potential of getting more support of all kinds from the community—media sponsorships, corporate sponsorships, ticket sales, word-of-mouth support, etc. The momentum and enthusiasm of John and the committee helped TCU find a new conference and raised visibility for what collegiate athletics could do for a city. "TCU: Your Home Team" became the theme, family ticket packages and incentives were created, and a pre-game carnival was launched with live entertainment to make tailgating more attractive for families. Pre-game and halftime entertainment was enhanced with parachute jumping and fireworks. All this together produced one of the biggest percentage increases in attendance in the country that year.

We learned that an integrated approach to marketing works. We developed coordinated themes, got everyone on the same page, segmented our market, and worked to develop active relationships. We developed sponsorships and partnerships, and, above all, we got the leadership of the Fort Worth to take some ownership of solving the problem with us. The process worked, and the benefits are still with us.

During this experience many were asking whether, since this kind of integrated approach to marketing athletics can be so effective, it could work for the university as a whole. The idea intrigued me so, with the help of then Chancellor William E. Tucker, I launched the TCU Integrated Marketing Task Force, a university-wide participatory team project to increase the number of student applications and raise TCU's visibility. Our enrollment was not down, but we were aware of the increased competition for good students and wanted to get ahead of any problem.

With the help of the current chancellor, Michael R. Ferrari, we expanded the effort and began to write and speak about what we were learning. What we learned at TCU in the last seven years comprises the primary research supporting this book. In the last four years I also traveled to more than 25 campuses and spoke on the subject of integrated marketing at countless conferences and seminars in the United States and abroad, taking what we learned here on the road. I visited extremely large public universities and small private colleges, and I visited medium-sized campuses—regional publics, top-quality privates, primary and secondary independent schools—in the United States, Canada, South America, the United Kingdom, and South Africa. Discussions with presidents, headmasters, faculties, deans, and advancement professionals during these travels enriched my understanding of the challenge of marketing the academy in today's competitive environment. Over this period of time, I have also dialogued via e-mail with countless individuals about the marketing issues on their campuses.

This book is intended, therefore, to be helpful to presidents, headmasters, vice presidents, trustees, deans, and department heads. It applies directly to the work of professionals in communications, public relations, media relations, publications, special events, admissions, financial aid, continuing education, alumni relations, fund raising and athletics. It should also be of interest to those working in student affairs, the business office, and the bookstore and to anyone else who makes contact with the people they serve.

I wish to acknowledge the influence of the following people and institutions on the ideas in this book: Stan Madden, Baylor University; Christopher Simpson, Indiana University (currently Simpson Communications, LLC); Fred Esplin, University of Utah; Ligeia Polidora, San Francisco State University; Susan Ruddy, University of Alaska; Lisa Grider, Seton Hall University (currently Graham Pelton Consulting); John McNamara, University of San Diego; Ann Millner, Weber State University; Bill Walker; Rutgers University; James Purcell, Santa Clara University; Lamie Umsted, Southeastern Oklahoma State University; Helen Ackerman, George Mason University; Barbara Castello, James Madison University; Patrick Lee, Pitzer College; Ed Ziegler, Rowan University; John Hitt, University of Central Florida; Carolyn Barnes; Texas Woman's University; Dawn Garrett, Freed-Hardeman University; Donna McElligott, Marboro College; Frank Albrighton, University of Birmingham (UK); Adrian Beney and Peter Slee, University of Durham (UK); Donna Renie, University of Cheltenham and Gloucester College

(UK); Victoria Collins, Memorial University of Newfoundland; Susan Montague, University of New Brunswick; Elaine Cadell, University of Saskatchewan; Johannes Hendrikz, University of Pretoria (South Africa); Julie Simon-Dronet, University of Louisiana at Lafayette; and John Thomas, Saint Mary's Hall.

Other influencers include John Lippincott and Deborah Bongiorno, Council for Advancement and Support of Education; Scott Levine and Elizabeth Scarborough, Carnegie Communications; Bob Sevier, Stamats Communications; Bob Johnson, Chair, American Marketing Association Annual Symposium on Marketing Higher Education; Dick Jones, Dick Jones Communications; Joanna Motion, CASE Europe; Nancy Raley, National Association of Independent Schools; Brenda Rouse, Henry Stewart Publications; Kristen Simpson, past editor of CURRENTS; Rob Moore and Donna Van De Water, Lipman Hearne; Neil Clark, Chair, National Small College Enrollment Conference; Norman Drummond and Ian Chisholm, Columba 1400 Leadership Centre (Isle of Skye, Scotland); and Michael Ferrari, Chancellor of Texas Christian University.

Above all I must express my deepest appreciation to the marketing and communication staff members at TCU who over the last seven years have helped me adapt and implement these marketing ideas. These people include Kelli Horst, Rick L'Amie, David Van Meter, Margaret Kelly, John Maddox, Victor Neil, Gorland Mar, Nancy Bartosek, Allie Regan, Tracy Syler-Doctson, Sandy Record, Chad Lorance, Tracy Bristol, Ben Alexander, Dee Dodson, Rick Waters, Allison Holt, Terri Gartner, Henri Etta Kilgore, and Nancy Styles. Others at TCU who played a significant role include Sandy Ware, Ray Brown, Barbara Herman, and Chuck Lamb.

Also I must express my appreciation to my wife Sterling, daughters Amy and Greta, sons-in-law Eric and Bill, and grandchildren Page, Lauren, and Will for their understanding and support as I traveled the world, missing weekends and cutting into vacations. I found out that the more one travels, the more important one's home becomes.

Marketing Is a Way of Thinking

This book is about how integrated marketing, participatory planning, and inspired leadership will revitalize and inspire institutional achievement. It will explain how to integrate the entire process of marketing and communication so that all units involved work effectively together in a coordinated way. It will describe how to design participatory planning processes that will enable all stakeholders to take ownership and become enthusiastic about helping move the institution ahead. And it will explain how to develop and motivate inspired leaders at the top and in other strategic places to play the most vital roles of all.

Saying the right things at the right time to the right people provides a personified, visible symbol of an enterprise moving forward and gets everyone else on the same page. All of this allows communications materials and campaigns to support leadership instead of trying to take its place—a critical factor in making institutions vital and exciting. Marketing the institution, then, is a process of orchestration, as well as a way of thinking.

Marketing as a way of thinking is not necessarily a way of commercializing. Indeed it need not be and should not be when applied to the academy. Rather it is a way of considering society's needs, the institution's academic program strengths, the experience of the total place, how learning is delivered, how it is all priced, and how the place is communicated—all at the same time. It is thus about establishing the necessary organizational processes that put everyone in the institution on the same page and plan coordinated steps to move it ahead.

... this mind-stretching new global economy has created a climate where institutions of all kinds have had to become a lot more competitive to thrive and, in some cases, survive.

ADAPTING THE ACADEMY TO CHANGE

Every moment in human history probably has felt like a time of incomprehensible change. No matter how slow progress may have actually been, those living at the time are likely to have felt that too much was happening too soon. But whatever the situation may have been in the past, change during the last decade of the 20th century and the beginning of the 21st century has by comparison has been staggering.

Change has come faster than most minds can really comprehend. A television- and image-dominated age has been to a large degree quickly reshaped by the Internet and digital revolution. Off-site communication by pay phone has given way to go-everywhere cell phones. And an almost comprehensible economy has given way to a new, more-difficult-to-understand economy based on digital technology and instant global connections. Indeed, the way business is conducted, war is waged, families function, careers develop, individuals communicate, politics is practiced, religion is understood, and values are shaped all changed in one way or another in most every part of the world in a very short period of time.

Obviously academic institutions are right in the middle of this revolutionary change. This is true not only because subject matters and teaching methods must adjust to dramatically new technology and rapid changes in subject-matter content, but also because this mind-stretching new global economy has created a climate where institutions of all kinds have had to become a lot more competitive to thrive and, in some cases, survive.

DEVELOPING A GLOBAL PERSPECTIVE

Indeed this new global economy, coupled with a climate of overwhelming communication clutter, requires institutions to take specific steps to be more effective in attracting the best students, raising enough money, and building a credible academic reputation. Although conditions in different parts of the world vary and the details of some situations differ, there is clearly a growing common need for academic institutions to become more systematic and professional in the way they understand and meet individual and social needs, and then communicate effectively and interactively the institution's benefits and strengths.

DEALING WITH PUBLIC CRITICISM

All of this also comes at a time when institutions in many parts of the world, including the United States, are coming under intense criticism. Some of that criticism is about quality—questioning faculty competency and educational relevance to this new world. Some of this criticism has focused on institutional policies and perspectives related to issues such as intercollegiate athletics costs and standards, practices in human-subject research, and concerns about substance abuse and crime on campus. Also, concern about increasing costs and related high tuition and fees has generated growing public criticism of overpricing the product.

THE CONCEPT OF INTEGRATION

This book is about how effective marketing can help institutions be competitive in the face of rapid worldwide changes. It argues that marketing is a way of thinking, not a way of commercializing. It is about how to integrate marketing activities throughout the whole institution and establish processes where everyone feels involved. It is also about what it will take to lead this kind of academic enterprise in the 21st century.

REVITALIZING INSTITUTIONS

This is a new world, no doubt about it. And this world will require institutions with clear missions, visions and values, effective marketing, clear communication, and inspired leadership. That's what marketing applied to the academy is all about. It is a way of thinking that engages everyone in shaping and communicating the organization.

An institution is truly effective only when everyone in it accepts some of the responsibility for its marketing. There are professionals, of course, who systematically contact and recruit prospective students, write and design materials, organize events, make fund-raising calls, work directly with the news media, and so forth. This is vital work that supports the marketing effort. But others lead it by standing out front and articulating the lead message or story. And still others play a vital role by never missing an opportunity to tell that story or to help solve a problem. Being an effective institution requires everyone to think about how the world and the educational needs of those the institution serves are changing. Indeed, all must play their parts as they meet and greet people going about their daily work. Integrated marketing helps establish institution-wide processes for getting the whole place involved and engaged.

ADVANCEMENT FOR THE 21ST CENTURY

The advancement profession has traditionally been seen to comprise three disciplines: fund raising, alumni relations, and communications. Some have referred to this as a "three-legged stool." Additionally, a single structural model incorporating these three disciplines is viewed as the best way to organize the functions in all institutions.

Today, changes in the marketplace are bringing about a new way of thinking both about the subject matter and the best way to organize the work. The subject matter is rapidly expanding with topics that demand stand-alone attention: *marketing* (with various ideas about integrating it and innovative thoughts about building relationships), *new media* (including the Internet, CDs, ideas about how the new economy works, and other technology innovations), and *research* (with more emphasis on market-segment-focused research, a more sophisticated approach to donor prospecting, and new approaches to online surveying). As for marketing, more and more advancement professionals are addressing ways to enhance its stature in the profession. And the need to become more competitive is also bringing it more to the forefront in total institutional planning.

Indeed, travels around the world reveal many emerging organizational structures. In today's competitive world, each institution's circumstances are clearly different and need to be taken into account when organizational charts are drawn. Different institutions have different histories, management styles, and corporate cultures. Size makes a difference. And the interests and talents of the president also determine what areas he or she wants reporting directly and how to organize teams and planning processes.

In many cases the traditional model still works best. But even here it is more important than ever for the person leading this division to have a big-picture perspective of all the disciplines and new subject-matter topics and to manage accordingly. Typically, the top person most often comes from a fund-raising background where the demands of this work and repeated campaigns cause overall student recruiting, alumni relations (other than annual fund raising), and reputation-building to go under-attended. The people in those areas then come to feel under-represented in overall planning and in the annual budgeting process.

Many new organizational structures are emerging. In some cases innovative approaches to creating task forces take the place of restructuring the administration. In other cases a separate marketing and communication division is formed, which may include units such as admissions and even the campus police. (This occurred at Baylor University, which viewed its police as a major factor in communication and "customer" relations.) Some institutions in both the UK and South Africa call the overall advancement division "marketing," which includes corporate partnership development activities as well.

Indeed, there are many right ways to organize this subject matter and its related professional work. These days each institution must understand its marketplace, competitive advantages, culture, and talents when it designs its approach to institutional advancement.

CHAPTER ONE

How Students, Fund Raising, and Media Markets Are Changing

This book is about how integrated marketing, participatory planning, and inspired leadership can revitalize institutions. It is also about change. Make no mistake: The economic and social environments in which academic institutions go about their business are changing worldwide.

THE HIGHER EDUCATION MARKETPLACE TODAY IS INTERNATIONAL

While it is true that the majority of students in most institutions come from within a few hundred miles, the new global economy and technology has changed the way everything works. We have gone from institutions that have study-abroad programs and a handful of international students to institutions where international is becoming a way of thinking.

Today, in addition to recruiting students abroad, faculty are taking a more international approach to their subject matter, scholars are increasingly traveling and working abroad, we are developing more international partnerships with various kinds of institutions and research organizations, and we are following our alumni and donors around the world. As the world becomes smaller for all of us, we are sharing what we are learning about recruiting students, raising money, and building reputation. Indeed, we are finding that intense interest in adapting marketing to the academy is developing in many parts of the world virtually at the same time. This book has been influenced by professional colleagues in the United States, Canada, Latin America, the UK, Europe, Australia, and South Africa.

In all these countries, the specific circumstances are different. For example, higher education students in the UK have recently begun to pay tuition. Students pay the same price regardless of which institution they attend. In the near future, when some institutions want to charge more than others, differential pricing will for the first time become an issue and thereby significantly change the approach to student recruiting. In South Africa the new democracy is making an advanced education possible for more people, but the system is going through a major adjustment period that has produced a whole new set of communication and fund-raising challenges. The situations are different, but the need for a new level of marketing and communication sophistication has arisen in both places at the same time. This is true in the other countries as well.

YET ANOTHER COMMUNICATION REVOLUTION

Society no sooner adjusts to one communication revolution than another comes along. When print was the dominant medium, its rational qualities tended to influence and even shape institutions and societies. Then television ushered in the world of imagery, and its emotional qualities tended to overpower the influence of print.

Indeed, people like H.A. Innis in *The Bias of Communication* and Marshall McLuhan in *The Medium Is the Massage* pointed out that when a new medium predominates, the way the world works tends to reorganize around it. During the shift from print to TV, people in general shifted in their preferences from the rational to the emotional. Yes, the world of images changed how families, politics, organized religion, the news business, and institutions function.

Now digital communication and the Internet enter the picture. Many think the Internet has already has replaced television as the dominant influence. Whether or not this is true overall, there is no doubt that it is already changing how institutions function, and it is taking the communication field into new areas of issues and concerns.

In the academy, for example, everyone sees what the Internet should do from a different point of view. And there is often a tug of war for editorial control between those in information services and those in communications. If you are a faculty member, you are likely to see the Internet primarily as a scholarship and interpersonal communication tool. Depending on where you are in the organization, you may also see it as a registration-management tool, a business-management tool, a research tool, an information-search tool, or a marketing and public relations tool. In fact it is all of these, and managing it requires an ability to satisfy all of these needs and perspectives.

In addition, there are different views on how to use the Web effectively. Some see it as heavy on design and pictures. These people tend to see the screen as more of a TV with expanded capabilities. Others see it as more of an information tool, a directory with links to vital data. Learning how to use it effectively from all of these perspectives is a challenge, to say the least. The truth is that it is a whole new medium with a little bit of all of the above, and integrating it into the advancement profession and the academic system as a whole is a revolutionary change for everyone.

A MORE SOPHISTICATED CONSUMER

The intense competition for students, money, and visibility is partly fueled by a more intelligent and sophisticated consumer. Higher education is merely responding to a larger change in society as a whole. Everyone today is a shopper.

More second- and third-generation college students are learning from their parents how to approach the admissions process. And everyone is getting more help from secondary-school counselors, teachers, and even independent consultants. The result is that prospective students and parents are shopping institutions more intelligently. They are no longer as intimidated by the fear of not getting in. Of course they are concerned about getting in to "good" schools, but they are a lot more aware of their options. Thus they apply to more schools and ask better questions. They are aware of financial-aid possibilities and are better equipped to compare institutions. And this process fuels the competitive environment.

Since more donors are involved with more than one institution, they are often involved in more than one comprehensive campaign. Even academic trustees may have divided loyalties because they also serve on symphony or opera boards, human-service boards, or museum boards. They may even serve on other university or school boards. Thus competition for their attention and money is intense. This situation calls for new initiatives, and some of those ideas are coming from the field of relationship marketing.

In the midst of this competitive situation, volunteers are calling for more visibility. They feel a greater need to be seen. As a consequence, everyone is competing for more news-media attention. Since faculty, staff, and students also want more prominence, new and more innovative marketing techniques are in demand. What can be done to get media attention? What can be done to bypass the news media and go directly to stakeholders and opinion leaders? Again marketing has some answers.

FOR-PROFIT EDUCATION AND DISTANCE LEARNING

The aggressive moves for-profit academies make these days challenge the entire educational world. Many believe that the academic quality and effectiveness of for-profit institutions will ultimately falter as commercial needs compromise educational mission. On the other hand, these enterprises bring some compelling features to the education marketplace, a marketplace that like all others functions largely on meeting needs.

First, for-profit enterprises offer convenience. They are situated in familiar locations convenient to the workplace. Next, their faculty has real-world experience. Yes, traditional academics point out how part-time faculty varies in quality and brings less interpersonal time to the educational process. They also point out how a life of research and scholarship enriches the learning process for students who come into contact with it. But for-profit institutions compensate by providing standardized course content, faculty training, and access to the faculty through technology. The educational experience is different. Many will continue to choose a more traditional campus setting, but these organizations meet a need and, as a result, will be shrinking the market for the rest.

Distance learning is a similar phenomenon. It offers convenience to both nontraditional and traditional students. It offers nontraditional students an opportunity to choose both place and time. Nontraditional students are usually more interested in basic information and degree completion than emotional growth and mentoring. And there are plenty of them. In some parts of the world, for example, South Africa, the distance learning enrollment of traditional institutions exceeds that of the on-campus student body.

Traditional students find distance learning attractive because they can mix traditional classes with one or two others that they can do in their own time and place. It also enhances a global perspective because a study-abroad student can also be enrolled in electronic courses via distance linkages. Thus the student can be on campus some of the time but not all the time.

The lesson here is that for-profit organizations and distance learning are meeting real student needs. The impact on the whole system will be large and permanent. Even though these developments will not eliminate the market for the traditional campus experience, they will shrink the overall market for these institutions. Marketing offers some tools to deal with these changes.

LIFELONG LEARNING

Continuing education is regarded differently on different campuses. Some see it as a central part of the mission, others as a very limited service to the community. But from a marketing perspective, it has incredible implications.

First of all, continuing education represents an opportunity for building critical partnerships in the community, not only with important individuals but with organizations as well. This opens many fund-raising, reputation-building, and traditional student-recruiting opportunities. When planning this curriculum, it is absolutely essential to clarify market targets so that relationship-building opportunities are not missed. In some cases, business and agency affiliations developed through continuing education enhance graduate programs and research.

Also, continuing education can play a role in donor cultivation and alumni family relationships. Opportunities to teach part-time credit or non-credit courses do a lot to cultivate and keep key people close to the institution. Guest-lecturing invitations help too. And, of course, career- and personal-enhancement courses provide great opportunities to keep entire alumni families involved. Some of these are serious study opportunities; others are pure adventures in ideas or just plain fun. Again, relationship-marketing tactics can help.

THE DISCOUNTING CONFUSION

Public opinion seems to hold that higher education and all levels of private education have overpriced themselves. But there is also the perception that for any product to have high quality it has to have a high price. Therefore academic institutions have tended to set a high price and then freely discount it. The problem is that now no one knows what a quality education should cost, and no one wants to pay the "sticker price." Certainly more sophisticated consumers know about all this and expect some level of discount. Hence the marketplace has created a very confused pricing situation.

Now institutions are trying to understand pricing better through research and trying to more effectively explain what they are doing. But it is challenging because these institutions are labor intensive, have very high salary costs, have to maintain very expensive facilities and campuses, and therefore have a hard time keeping their increases in line with standard-of-living increases. And high tuition doesn't even cover the entire cost. Endowment earnings and gifts contribute as well. With pricing such an issue, marketing tools can also provide needed analysis, policy decision-making information, and communication strategies.

DEALING WITH DIVERSITY

Diversity is also a large and complicated issue on campuses. A more diverse student body and faculty is the goal of many institutions, largely because of the need to address the imbalance created by socioeconomic factors. But accomplishing this is not easy. And demographic shifts in some areas, such as California and Texas, are adding both to the problem and to the urgency.

Diversity has many dimensions, and educational institutions want to be diverse in all of them. When diversity is considered, all of these factors apply: ethnic, economic, gender, religious, cultural, educational, and more. There is always a reason why the people who are on campus are there, and why those who are not on campus are not. Attracting those who have not previously found the place attractive always takes more time and effort and money than anyone expects. Thus many campuses have failed to make progress. But marketing can help with developing a strategic plan of action.

INSTITUTIONS AT RISK

More and more institutions are likely to face hard times as competition increases for students, money, and visibility. Even top-tier schools are likely to feel the pressure.

Defined solely in traditional academic terms, there are only a certain number of "best" students. Top-tier schools will therefore increasingly compete with each other, while second-tier schools will make stronger and stronger cases to attract some of these students to their institutions. More sophisticated consumers will look for quality in many places and, over time, may modify their behavior. As more and more schools develop better-defined quality niches, consumer market behavior will gradually change. Top-tier schools, too, will have to make their cases in a more sophisticated way.

Schools below the top tier will feel most of the pressure, however. They will have to be much more effective in strategic marketing, something in which they have little experience. Indeed, most presidents have some experience in the fund-raising and alumni relations aspects of advancement. They picked this up over time as they moved from academic leadership into more central responsibilities. But when it comes to combining all of this into a more complex and integrated approach to student recruiting and overall institutional reputation building, very few have much background or experience. Doing all of this with scarce resources is indeed a challenge, but integrated marketing can show how designing a better process can lead to strong improvements in all these areas.

Of course, some schools will be fighting for their very survival. For these it is important to note that the smaller the institution, the better integrated marketing can work. Smaller schools can more readily define their special competitive advantage, more clearly target markets for it, and more effectively get everyone on the same page and involved with the quest. It is not all about money. It is also about mobilizing the troops.

CHAPTER TWO

The Thinking Process

In the academy, marketing should not be commercializing. Marketing is a way of thinking. Certainly when it comes to academic enterprises, we are not talking about turning university campuses into shopping centers. Indeed, we are not talking about anything that will cheapen the academic world or diminish its stature. On the contrary, we are talking about the kind of analysis that demands quality and reveals when it is not there.

Marketing is not promotion. It is more than communicating the programs and services you already offer. It is a way of thinking about the programs you offer, the price you charge for them, the places and mechanisms for their delivery, and the way you communicate them—all at the same time. It is about setting up processes that enable these kinds of conversations and this kind of planning. And it is about getting everyone in the enterprise to assume a role in making it happen.

Marketing requires thinking strategically. It requires clear targets and an ability to put into place the progressive actions that will reach them. In order to have clear targets, an institution must have a clear mission, vision, and values.

MISSION

Yes, I know you are tired of hearing about mission. But a clear mission statement is the single most important factor in effective institutional or services marketing. Everything else follows from it. It is the set of concepts that define everything else.

Your mission is the specific reason why your organization went into business. What did it go into business to do? Fill in the blank: "My institution came into being in order to ___________." Go back to your organization's historical roots; study the founders and the circumstances that gave birth to this enterprise. Why did they go to the trouble? What compelled them to do it? Look for the emotions they felt and the language they used.

Now assemble a representative group from around campus to develop the words—a statement of "25 words or less" that everyone can remember and easily repeat. This is critical. It becomes the primary mechanism for getting everyone on the same page. Since it will become the primary mechanism for motivating people to get involved, it has to have meaning but it must also be brief. Both are important. When the statement is ready, release it for comment and reactions. Make editorial adjustments as appropriate.

After you've given people enough time to express their opinions, start rolling it out in materials, meetings, and virtually all communications. Some institutions might also want to involve trustees and key volunteers. Keep in mind that while all might not agree on the exact words, if everyone has input and the statement truly reflects founding purposes, people eventually will rally to its support. Chapter 8 discusses how to build an internal marketing program around this new sense of mission.

Once an institution has a clear mission statement, everyone begins to measure everything that is done and every decision that is made according to whether or not it will fulfill the mission. This is the heart of strategic thinking and the heart of marketing.

VISION

If your mission is what your institution was founded to do, then your vision is what it wants to become. Vision must be anchored in mission or it won't ring true, won't seem possible. It will ring hollow. But if a visionary statement extends directly from mission, it can be quite challenging, indeed inspiring. You might even want to become the best in the world at what you do. Such a statement, however, will only seem credible if your mission is clear to begin with and is relatively focused and intensely urgent.

Vision is as important as mission in marketing services or institutions because it provides emotional fuel and drive for making things happen. Mission makes people feel connected and satisfied, but vision rallies the troops and makes them achieve. Vision is what establishes the feeling of forward movement and, as such, it is critical to bringing about a feeling of revitalization. It stimulates new levels of achievement and distinction. This is what the integrated marketing process has the potential to do.

VALUES

Values clarification is the primary element in building corporate culture. A shared sense of institutional culture is critical to teamwork, which makes the journey to distinction satisfying. Unless making good things happen is satisfying, people won't do it over the long term. When teamwork and participatory processes break down, organizations plateau and forward movement stalls. Rumors intensify and complaints about communication and leadership abound. Organizations become dysfunctional when values are lost. Then leaders either need to do something to generate an "it's-a-new-day" feeling—or they need to be replaced. It's as simple as that.

Identifying and listing values can also begin with an examination of the organization's roots. The values list is often very close to the mission statement because values are often about the same thing—not what the organization was founded to do but how it intends to do it. Founding language often expresses values too. Mission, vision, and values are all essential points of departure for building a marketing initiative.

Marketing as a way of thinking also begins with four key marketing ideas. There are more to follow, of course. But the way to learn to think strategically about marketing after you clarify mission, vision, and values is to understand *positioning, relationship building, segmentation,* and *integration*.

POSITIONING

Marketing is ultimately about giving your institution a competitive advantage. It begins with a frank and open understanding of your institution's strengths and its weaknesses. Assuming your strengths have grown from your mission, your task is to plan how to maximize and supplement them. You have a more complicated and perhaps impossible problem if your strengths don't match your mission. Weaknesses often lead to the hardest part of the marketing process: the need to eliminate activities that are not central to the mission.

Positioning involves clarifying strengths so as to establish a distinct place among your competitors for what you do: your mission. It is not merely stating the distinction; it is creating a position in *the prospect's mind* for what you do. Therefore, it must take into account your strengths and those of your competitors and state your case so that the prospect sees and values it. The language needs to be more than clear; it has to have meaning and distinction for the prospect. We sometimes call this a "niche" in the marketplace.

The best discussion of positioning is in the now-classic book, *Positioning*, by Al Ries and Jack Trout. In our over-communicated world, it is difficult to make a place for your institution in anyone's mind. It is difficult to be heard, let alone be understood, in today's communication clutter. Ries and Trout point out that the best way to get into someone's mind is to be the first at something. But being first is becoming harder and harder to do. How can your institution be the first?

It is difficult to be heard, let alone be understood, in today's communication clutter.

It is not enough to be better than your competition; you need to differentiate yourself. You must select a focused concept that is most likely to get through the clutter. Avis car rental made a successful distinction out of being number two: They try harder. The concept filled a hole in the consumer's mind. But now Avis can never be number one. Once Seven Up determined it would never be the number-one soft drink, it created a new industry category, the "Uncolas," and instantly became number one on that list. How might this apply to your institution?

Name is important. Most institutional marketers these days feel that the better your institution's name is known, the higher quality people think it is. Therefore, a name that sticks in the mind and is easy to remember is very valuable. A long and difficult name is a liability. How can you make your name an asset? A name that stands for something is best. How can you associate the emotional feeling of your mission, vision, and values with it each time you communicate?

Ries and Trout point out that sometimes "you position the country, not the airline." Where your institution is located may be what causes it to stick in the mind. Alaska, Newfoundland, Charleston, and New Orleans, for example, may have compelling positioning possibilities for institutions. Does this idea apply to your institution?

Diversification, however, is certainly not the answer to positioning. "Best comprehensive university in the area" is not a position. You need a differentiating distinction that will have meaning in the mind of the prospect. For many institutions this distinction sometimes may be difficult, even impossible, to find. But the search process itself has a very positive effect on building a team and almost always makes communication more precise and effective. It makes for more interesting planning meetings and retreats. The search should be seen as an evolving process that does produce positive short-term communication improvements, even if true clarity of distinction seems to be a longer-term challenge.

RELATIONSHIP BUILDING

A bonded relationship may be your best competitive advantage. You can start a new program that, for a while, may provide a competitive advantage. But your competition will do the same and diminish that advantage. You can do the same thing with price, a more convenient location, and so forth. But, here too, your competition can match your initiative and diminish your advantage. When you build a relationship, however, it is far more difficult for your competitors to diminish your advantage.

People feel better doing business in places where they are familiar with the surroundings and know the people. They are often willing to pay a premium for that feeling. The bond can be compelling enough to force competitors to spend a lot of time and money to weaken it. They actually have to first build a better relationship with that prospect to do it. So building relationships becomes the focus of a truly effective marketing effort.

When an institution begins thinking this way, it changes what people do with their time and how they do it. All student recruiting activities and materials now focus on building relationships that ultimately establish the feeling, "I just like this place and these people better." The office of communication thinks less about mass communication and broadcasting and more about building relationships with stakeholders and opinion leaders. This changes what they write and where they send it. The whole organization becomes aware that when a prospect comes to campus, he or she will leave feeling either attached to the place or distant from it. Only those who feel the relationship will come back, as students, as faculty, as staff, or as donors. How to build these relationships is a strategic thinking and planning process and is the most important marketing challenge of all.

SEGMENTATION

"Know your audience" is the familiar message of the public-speaking teacher. Know their needs when you begin your talk, and tell them in a straightforward manner how what you say will meet their needs. Meet them where they are and lead them from there.

The idea of marketing upsets some people in the academy because they think it means giving the students just what they want, and that teachers and staff know better what students need than they do. But it is not that at all. Marketing does not mean that you simply meet people's needs. You often end up satisfying needs that people did not know they had. You take them far beyond their expectations. But you had to begin where you found them and know what they think they need in order to meet and surpass those needs. Organizing the market into specific audiences is what we in marketing call "segmentation." By studying these segments we learn about needs and how to communicate more effectively.

When I bought my last car, the salesman asked me what I was looking for, what features I would like to have. I told him. He showed me cars that met my needs. But as I drove the cars, I became acquainted with features that exceeded my expectations. To be sure, he had to show me products that would meet my perceived needs. But what he showed me also took me far beyond those needs.

This is what I call the "wow factor," and educational institutions certainly can and should be providing that. We attract students by meeting their perceived needs, but then the faculty and staff take them far beyond those needs to experiences and satisfactions they never imagined. I still drive around in the rain to show people how my windshield wipers adjust themselves to the intensity of the rainfall. It was a feature I never knew existed, and now I guess I will need to have it from now on!

Segmentation is a way to organize your market so that you can study each segment separately and interact appropriately. It improves marketing research because it is more focused. Questions become more precise, and the information learned is easier to apply. Communication can then focus more on the audience and be more interactive because the channels within segments are usually more direct and provide more interactive possibilities. In other words, everything you do becomes more informed and produces better results. Identifying, categorizing, and prioritizing segments becomes an important strategic part of marketing.

INTEGRATION

Student recruiting, communications, fund raising, alumni relations, athletics marketing, and so forth have traditionally been located in various different divisions of academic institutions that often report to different administrative officers. They have tended to set their own goals and operate their own shops with very little interaction or coordination. When the world was less competitive, this seemed to be satisfactory.

But in recent years competition has created need for greater coordination. Suddenly being on the same page with respect to goals and message seems critical. Since the intensity made possible by orchestrating all of these human and financial resources also seems critical, institutions are thinking more about how to integrate their marketing efforts.

The easiest and sometimes most effective approach is to create a task force involving these people. I discuss how to do this in Chapter 5. Some institutions are also considering restructuring to bring at least some of these units together. How to do this, as I mentioned before, is very much an institution-specific issue that must take into account management styles, organizational history, and the interests and preferences of the president. But some form of integration is essential if an academic institution is to improve its marketing effectiveness and achieve a sense of revitalization.

An integrated marketing program also calls for integrating communication tools, which is critical to improving the effectiveness of money already being spent throughout the institution. Integrated planning determines the communication objectives appropriate to the institution's objectives and priorities and then encourages the use of all the tools necessary to achieve them. It plans all communication with more of a campaign approach wherein public relations, advertising, and other marketing initiatives all work together, not separately and independently. I'll discuss this in more detail later.

In the final analysis, integrating marketing people and functions facilitate setting institutional goals and priorities, rather than allowing each of these units to go in their own directions. And it provides the forum for getting everyone on the same page with respect to mission, vision, values, competitive advantage, institutional strengths and weaknesses, graphics standards, and more. When you add the appropriate academic and student affairs people to the mix, you have put in place a process whereby programs, pricing, program delivery, and communication can all be considered at the same time.

CHAPTER THREE

Adapting the Basics of Marketing

The standard introduction to the basics of marketing is a definition of the four P's: product, place, price, and promotion. These days many have substituted other words. But for the purpose of adapting basic thinking to the academy, these concepts work just fine.

PRODUCT

In higher education—or in other schools for that matter—we talk about products at both ends of the enterprise. We talk about the *products that our consumers buy*, and we talk about the *products we produce* and distribute to the world. From a marketing perspective, it is important to be clear about both.

With respect to the products that prospective students and parents buy, there is some differentiation between undergraduate prospects and prospective graduate students. Because institutions typically regard their undergraduate marketplace as their bread and butter, they allocate most marketing resources and efforts to shaping institutional identity and messages in that general direction. However, within that framework other marketing efforts are also aimed in other directions—at graduate students, donors, and alumni, among others. In some cases, institutions will be thinking more about these other markets than about undergraduates. Clarifying all of this is the first step in analytical thinking.

Within the undergraduate orientation, there are two other points of clarity: Do prospective students and parents buy primarily the institution itself? Or do they buy specific programs within it? There is some disagreement on this point and, since the answer varies from person to person and circumstance to circumstance, marketing planning must simultaneously address both.

With respect to the institution as a whole, the question is related to overall institutional identity and prestige. What does the prospect think he or she will get by associating with this place? Is it academic prestige? Is it social prestige? Is it the "in" place to be? Is it exciting associations with other creative and/or intellectual people? Is it an exciting social life? Is it a place where they can feel free of parentalism? Or a place where personal help is readily available? Is it a place with lots of diversity to experience? Other cultures? New ways of thinking? Or does it offer the comfort of being around others mostly like themselves? Prospects are trying to make an identity and emotional match. When they review marketing materials, they are trying to visualize themselves in the picture. Reading the words, they're trying to answer the question, "Can I see myself in the place?" Words and design combined have to clarify what kind of place it is.

You cannot communicate the place as you imagine it to be and succeed. You must come pretty close to communicating what it really is. Some degree of exaggeration, of course, is expected, but products and services must be verifiable. The communication must ring true to the consumer. If not, you will either lose the prospect during the campus visit or after the freshman year. If you are not satisfied with what your analysis reveals about your identity, you need to strengthen it—and that takes time.

In the world of services marketing, the product actually exists in the prospect's mind. You are what they perceive you to be. When you add a building, add new faculty, or raise your price, you may be improving quality, but it will only count in the marketplace if it changes the image of what you are in the prospect's mind. And that will take time, aggressive communication, and visionary leadership.

This is why it is so important to take an integrated approach to marketing. If you are not satisfied with your identity, it rarely is a communication problem alone. It almost always requires onboard administrators, dynamic leadership, and product adjustments to accomplish. The only way this can happen is to have processes in which all the right people work on the problem together.

This does not mean you cannot exaggerate at all. With some careful and restrained exaggeration, you can actually influence the development of the place. This is called a self-fulfilling prophecy, and it can work when your communication reinforces vision and is forward looking, inspiring, and self-confident, and therefore motivates the troops. But leading with too much rhetoric quickly becomes lying, and then you have crossed a very important line. This is the line between truth and lying, between integrity and dishonesty. And when prospects cannot verify your claims, you fail—just like that.

Research is an important factor in product development and communication, and I will talk a lot more about it in Chapter 7. Suffice it to say here that survey research is critical in the process of determining how your prospects actually see you. In marketing, that is the only thing that matters. What you are is what they think you are. Later, in follow-up focus groups, you ask the question: "Did you find what our materials and recruiters said you would find?"

The next aspect of product analysis relates to academic and co-curricular programs: What academic programs do you offer? How do prospects perceive them? What characteristics distinguish them? What factors make your journalism or engineering or history program special?

How much personal attention do students get? Academic reputation? Job placement? What are your outstanding academic programs?

This last question is difficult to answer internally for political reasons. Every department wants to think its program is excellent and, to some extent, you are recruiting students for all of them. But you must answer the question to succeed in the reputation-building aspect of marketing. A university's overall prestige is generally shaped by the visibility of its centers of excellence, and all who plan and market the school must agree about what they are. This clarification is especially important for those communicators, largely in the public relations area, who focus on building reputation. For public relations can consistently succeed only if it highlights true performance and excellence. Reputation building must always operate on the principle that centers of excellence will get more attention. Chapter 9 discusses how offices of communication can deal with this reality.

Programs in the student affairs area are important to marketing as well. Most play roles in helping students decide if they can see themselves in this setting. Specifically, new-student orientation, housing and lifestyle elements, job placement, physical fitness, and sports opportunities are important. Parents are interested in details about campus safety, health services, and the availability of counseling. They want to know how the institution will respond in a crisis. All these programs have a lot to do with the experience of the place, which is a critical factor in college selection.

PLACE

Place in marketing really means distribution—how the product or service is delivered. In education, that means classrooms and other learning environments, use of technology in delivering courses, the overall campus setting, and other services. Let me begin by continuing the previous discussion of "experienced place."

One of the most important insights in marketing institutions is that there are two ways to see the physical place. One is the actual physical setting as seen through the eyes. The other is the place that is remembered as an experience after a visit. The latter is far more important than the former.

The more attractive a campus looks at first sight the better. Green lawns, flowerbeds, attractive meeting areas, statues, and artwork all come together with mental images of academic reputation and other factors to form a single impression of the likely experience. But not very far into a visit an even stronger force emerges, one that shapes the lasting impression.

Prospects may first encounter a police officer while trying to park the car. Then ask a student or staff member for directions. Then see the admissions receptionist. Then see an array of staff, faculty, and students as the experience unfolds. Each encounter generates an impression, and each impression contributes to a whole perception that supersedes the physical campus impression every time. The reason some prestigious institutions with squalid residence halls are successful is because something about the experienced place is more powerful than the physical reality.

A very important aspect of the marketing plan is the development and management of the place the prospect experiences, a process that involves all of the public-contact people wherever they may be on campus. Sometimes it means organized customer-service training. It must always mean strong communication between and among all those who come into contact with visitors. While this is easy to neglect and difficult to accomplish, the marketing process must simply persevere until this is accomplished.

Classrooms and laboratories are important too. Many institutions have let these lag. They look ancient. They lack technology. Worse yet, more and more prospective students come from high schools that have more up-to-date learning environments than the universities they are considering. This is not to say that conventional environments are not important. They are.

Since, in the final analysis, prospects must make a connection between themselves and the kind of experience they imagine will take place in these settings, the way the physical setting produces an exciting experience should be the focus of marketing communications.

Distance learning, more of a factor in some places than others, has two roles. Where entire degree programs are offered, convenience is the hook and working and otherwise-occupied adults are the major markets. The other is where online courses are combined with classroom-based courses for traditional students. Of course, online courses for distance learners are a completely separate marketing issue. Some institutions see this as a major marketing opportunity, and others will not. This is a very institution-specific decision, and it will be a wise one for only some. Developing any new product or opening a new market always takes more time and more money than anyone expects. The lesson from industry is that you do this only if you are fully committed to carrying it out completely. It is a major decision for a traditionally committed institution to make.

Online courses for traditional students are another matter, however. Prospective students live in a multi-technology environment in which it is common practice to combine live experiences with virtual ones. It simply won't seem like the real world if technology is not used in this matter. Of course, this is where the need for technology training for faculty can come directly from the institution's marketing analysis—still another reason why the integrated approach that has the right people participating in the discussion is so important. It's just a fact of life today: In order to meet consumers where they are and to meet the needs they perceive they have, faculty and staff must know and use technology—at least in the courses and transactions where it clearly provides efficiency and interactive advantages.

In order to meet consumers where they are and to meet the needs they perceive they have, faculty and staff must know and use technology.

PRICE

From a marketing perspective, the worst reason in the world to raise the price is because you need the money. Price is a very important strategic aspect of the whole marketing mix. It relates to product perception and to perceptions of prestige as well.

What we are really talking about is *perceived value*. When there is a balance between the perceived value of what is being received and what is being paid, there is no price objection. When the balance is off, there is price objection and the customer walks. A set of factors make how price really functions for higher education and most other schools very difficult to understand.

- First, there is the public perception that higher education and many independent schools are overpriced. Wherever you are in the pricing range, many in your specific marketplace will think you are already overpriced.
- Second, even while they object to higher education costs overall, most of these same people think schools that are not high priced cannot be very good. This leads to the practice of quoting a high "sticker price" but discounting it for many.
- Third, the overall scholarships and financial aid to provide this discount have everyone confused with respect to what a good education should cost.
- Fourth, few even care to understand that consumers don't ever pay what an education actually costs. Donors and friends contribute so that students only pay a portion.

- Fifth, fewer still appreciate why costs for a labor-intensive institution with expensive libraries to sustain, technology to continually update, and vast grounds and buildings to maintain consistently increase faster than the standard of living. After all, it's not what higher education costs but the value perceived by the consumer that matters.

All of this makes price-setting decisions very complex. What's more, there is a disconnect between the institutions people *think* theirs competes with and the ones it *actually* competes with. When asked to name its competitors, people inside and outside an institution often name many that *they would like to be competing with*. But a marketing analysis may reveal that *actual* competitors are a different set of institutions. And when setting price, you must compare yourself to your actual rivals, even if your longer-range plan is to compete with your aspirant institutions. Some institutions learn the hard way. When they increase their price because they thought they were a lower-cost institution on the list of schools *they thought they were competing with*, they found out they were actually a higher-priced school on the list *they were actually competing with*.

With respect to pricing, your product is what consumers perceive it to be and its price category is based on what your price has been. To change price too fast can confuse and therefore lose them. Repositioning to a more prestigious category in the consumer mind requires gradual price increases, specific improvements in products, aggressive communication, and enough time for consumers to redefine the way they see you. Sometimes it requires enough time and communication to allow whole new consumers to consider you. Pricing is a complex and sticky business, and more research is needed on elasticity before we can be sure about what to do. Think carefully about all of the above factors before you act. Then you can at least make a more informed judgment about raising or adjusting tuition and fees. More about this in Chapter 7 where I talk about research.

PROMOTION

The problem is that when many people hear the word *marketing*, they think you mean *promotion*. But when we talk about marketing, it should now be clear that we are talking about programs, distribution, and pricing as well. Promotion is only one-fourth of the mix, and even then we seldom use that term. Today we always use the broader more inclusive term *communication* and we talk about *integrated marketing communication*.

In the professional fields of public relations, advertising, and marketing, there is a lot of debate about which tools are the most effective. Public relations practitioners argue in favor the "third-party endorsement" of the news media, often claiming that it is more effective than advertising. Advertising people argue for their power, direct marketers argue theirs, and so forth. But when you step back and look at the big picture, your real task is to set institutional marketing goals and then design the communication plan best-suited to achieve those goals. The plan will almost always be a campaign-style assortment of all of the tools, each one chosen for its particular strength and all of them coordinated to pull together in the same direction. Compatible in message and style, they will together have more intensity and impact. This is what we mean by integrated marketing communication, and this is still another reason why integrating the marketing planning process is so critical. By going through this exercise, many institutions can produce a lot more impact from the money that they are already spending.

Remember my point about relationships being your most potent competitive advantage? Integrated marketing communication is your most potent tool for building relationships, but implementing it requires most traditional offices of communication to change rather dramatically the way they go about their daily work. More about all this appears in Chapter 9.

FEATURES OR BENEFITS

The differentiation of features from benefits is always part of a discussion of marketing basics. It's very basic but very important because even seasoned marketing communications keep falling into the trap.

Features are the programs and services that are offered. On an automobile, features include the radio, electric windows, etc. Just listing and describing them is of no use to consumers if they don't see any benefit to them. And you can't talk persuasively about benefits unless you know a lot about the consumer's needs. Just as marketing must be translated to the academy, features must be translated—or connected—as benefits to the consumer.

Often, benefits are often obvious; the benefits of a car radio or electric windows are obvious. But benefits are not always obvious, and the obvious ones may not be the truly compelling ones. In the case of education, the benefits may be obvious, but a compelling and creative description of the full range of benefits might forge the compelling connection with the prospect that makes the difference. Instead of putting so much creative effort into new ways of showing and describing programs and services, it may be more effective to put that creative effort into delving deeper into the benefits.

IMAGE AND REPUTATION

How does all this relate to building reputation? What do we mean when we say an institution has a good image or a bad image? While all of the above is critical to shaping reputation, even more important is what the decision makers are or are not doing and how that is perceived inside and outside the institution.

Some think the way publications and advertisements look and what they say establish image. These people have a visual or picture idea of what an institutional image is. But image is really what people are saying about you. "I've heard that place is really in trouble these days." Or "Those people out there really know what they're doing. That place is really taking off." Image is established more by the perceived behavior of institutional leaders than by its materials. A lot of marketing planning therefore must involve making exciting things happen and getting the right people to talk about them.

Traditionally, selectivity is the primary symbol of educational quality. But more sophisticated consumers determine how selective so-called selective institutions really are based on a whole array of factors, including teaching effectiveness, job placement, class size, and delivery on promises.

If leaders seem dysfunctional or inept, the best materials in the world will ring hollow. Any marketing initiative launched by a massive mailing and widespread advertising campaign will fall silent in time if it is not led by exciting institutional leaders with dynamic ideas. It can look artificial if it's out there alone. It takes both the leadership saying the right things to the right people at the right time and an integrated marketing communication program to support and reinforce them. That is the way it must work, or a strong image cannot be built and sustained.

A marketing plan must provide specific roles to institutional leaders. The president must be out there visibly delivering the message to opinion leaders in each priority market segment. Key cabinet members and deans must be on-message, too. Talented faculty and staff must be asked to play a support role inside and out. If the integrated process has been properly inclusive, key people will already be on board. You just need to define their roles and ask them. All this human performance activity has more to do with image development than anything else. Get everyone on the same page and motivated to tell the story, and they will tell the same story in different words from different perspectives. The public perception will follow: "This place in on the move."

A MATTER OF QUALITY

Quality is the only thing that sells. In education, you cannot at any price say, "Well, you get what you pay for." But the way many consumers define quality today may be different than the way many in the academy define it.

Traditionally, selectivity is the primary symbol of educational quality. If your school is hard to get into, it must be good. Selectivity is still an issue for many consumers; it clearly carries a perception of quality. But more sophisticated consumers determine how selective so-called selective institutions really are based on a whole array of factors, including teaching effectiveness, job placement, class size, and delivery on promises. Upon closer analysis, some selective institutions are not really that selective, and many of those have a long way to go in the area of service delivery. Quality is critical, but education can no longer just claim it. The proof is in the pudding, and the consumer is examining the pudding.

BEST OF SHOW OR BEST OF BREED?

All of this leads to two questions:

- What claim can I make?
- How should my claim be rated with others?

Traditionally, consumers put all institutions on one big list; as institutions improve, they move up on the list. Some lists are broken down into public or private, large or small, national or local. But institutions move up or down on the list based on the same standard criteria.

What does an institution need to do to move up on the list? And what does moving up a slot or two really do for you? It takes a lot of money and time and effort to move ahead of the other guy, especially when the other guy is working to move up as well. Some institutions may want to consider the Uncola route: Define your own industry category so that you can be number one on it. That may seem deceitful, but it really isn't. In fact, it's great institutional marketing. It means that you have examined your roots, clarified your mission, defined real strengths based on substantial analysis, and are clear about what you are really good at doing. "Best of breed" may be the way for many institutions to go, even if defining it will take a lot of time and effort.

OTHER BASIC CONCEPTS

Basic concepts discussed previously that need to be adapted to the academy include

- The fundamental idea that segmenting the market facilitates more effective information gathering and interactive communication
- The practice of analyzing your competitors to clarify your competitive advantage; the intellectual exercise of positioning your institution—not by describing it more precisely but by finding a unique place for it in the mind of your prospects
- The fact that sometimes positioning leads to marginal differentiation, which involves adding something to make your product or service different and then claiming that the difference makes it better

Clarifying your market position, or niche, involves answering these questions:

- Who do you serve?
- Who do you want to serve?
- Is it worth the time and money to change who you serve?
- What are your real strengths?
- Who do you aspire to be like?
- Is being like them really more desirable than finding your significant difference?

Other key concepts include the whole idea of *integration*, focus on *relationship building*, the necessity of using *creative teams*, and the absolute necessity and power of *dynamic leadership*. There is more ahead on all of this.

CHAPTER FOUR

Taking a More Strategic Approach to Communication

Mass media have always been inefficient forms of communication. For all practical purposes, there is a one-way flow of information, a situation with many shortcomings when it comes clarifying messages and building relationships. But communication evolved from handwritten texts to the printing press to the capability for mass communication. For a period of time, mass communication dominated all human enterprise. After all, it had been established that if you wanted to have influence, you had to know how to use the dominant media.

With the emergence of the Internet and digital technology, communication evolution entered a new stage. Now capabilities emerged to permit communication with many individuals one person at a time. This technology had the potential for audience segmentation and two-way interaction, and it would still reach large numbers of people. The more the Internet expanded and technology use grew, the more communicators began to pronounce the death of mass communication.

Certainly, television would continue to have great influence, but it would gradually make room for this powerful new influence—just as print and radio made room for television. History teaches that when a new medium becomes dominant the others don't die, but they do adopt different roles with somewhat reduced influence.

There are some interesting implications here for strategic thinkers who are trying to apply the concepts of integrated marketing. When your task is to segment your market and build relationships, you are naturally attracted to media that will allow you to do exactly that. But you are also aware that all media tools have their place in the mix, their unique strengths and weaknesses. Taking a more strategic approach to communication planning becomes essential. What, then, have we learned from research and practice about how communications works that we can apply to our planning?

PRINT

Print requires organization and structure, and it is more effective when it is structured in three parts: beginning, body, and conclusion. The beginning says what you are going to tell them, the body lays it out, and the conclusion tells them what you told them. Within the body, it's more effective to follow a rational organizational scheme and not attempt to convey too much information. Usually people will not be able to remember more than four or five points, and even then the points have to be reinforced and repeated several times. Print, therefore, has a rational and linear quality that appeals most to people with intellectual preferences.

RADIO

Even though radio began to edge out newspapers as the dominant medium in the 1930s and '40s, it had to quickly assume a new role with the emergence of television in the '40s and '50s. Radio really found distinction as a mobile medium. Music became its forte, along with headline-length information. When cell phones made interaction with the mobile public more feasible, conversation-type radio programs made permanent inroads as well. Radio is for those on the go, and it particularly appeals to auditory learners—people who comprehend better when they hear it.

TELEVISION

Television is an emotional medium. Its images assault the senses and produce emotional responses. Television viewers receive more feelings and impressions than hard information. It tends to seem more real than it is. It selects images from various places and puts them together into a whole picture that is never exactly the same as reality. Every television picture is a montage of images spliced together, so that when you later see an event you have attended on television it always looks different. Each director will select different shots and angles, so different programs will look different from each other. And yet the images look so real that you feel you are really there.

In fact, television does not like details. The more details a program contains, the more boring the program seems to become. The tendency is to show pictures and to emphasize human feelings and responses. The medium is at its best when its emotional qualities are emphasized. The natural qualities of the medium tend to encourage emotional drama and discourage complicated intellectual examination.

THE INTERNET

The Internet is a whole new ballgame. It is a combination of print and pictures that, in this context, have new communication qualities. In the end, the Internet is an information-search medium. Ease of finding what you are looking for becomes its most important feature. Early beliefs that pictures should dominate a homepage are yielding to the belief that the homepage should look more like the front page of a newspaper. Displayed in three or four columns, the home page should contain a relevant picture or two, but it should not be dominated by beautiful design. It needs to look like a well-thought-out directory with clear linkages to what its users want to know. Therefore, you do have to know what users want to know and deliver them quickly to it. Since it is not an electronic picture brochure, professionals have to learn new ways of thinking to use it well.

THE NEWS

It is interesting, then, that television has become such a powerful news medium. Network and cable television news programs dominate the news business enough to influence how newspapers function as well. Even though newspapers add more detail and appeal to the more intellectual side of consumers, many newspapers have become much more visual and headline-oriented as they struggle to appeal more to a television-influenced audience. It's ironic that at a time when an informed public is most critical to the world, the dominant news medium—television—is less suited to intellectual pursuits and more likely to favor highly charged emotional drama.

IMPACT ON AUDIENCES

Experience teaches us that most people seem to favor emotion. But not all do. This has to be taken into account when segmenting audiences and selecting media. Families have changed. They tend to watch television and play computer games more as they interact with each other less. The TV room has become the place where communication clutter rules, leading most people to be confused about what is really happening in the world. Watching the Vietnam War on television, in the end, confused more than enlightened.

Television's impact carries to the workplace as well. People are more emotional here too. They want to have their feelings taken into account. They want to participate in the issues that affect them. They want to have visible, star-like leaders and to feel connected to them. In the end, they want immediate satisfaction and gratification—conflicts that are quickly resolved and rewards that are quickly delivered.

Audiences, then, are shaped by the medium they most often consume, and each medium has its own characteristics. When communicating with these consumers, you need to understand their emotional-versus-intellectual foundation and know their media preferences. In addition, you need to think through the actual communication process between sender and receiver.

HOW THE COMMUNICATIONS PROCESS WORKS

The person sending a message actually encodes it. To simplify the illustration, let's say an individual says or writes a word. What he or she is really doing is making a noise or writing some letters. That noise or those letters have a meaning to the receiver. The meaning is not actually sent from sender to receiver, but rather it is the sum total of the receiver's experience previously related to the noise or letters.

For example, I say "dog." One receiver may think happy thoughts imagining a cute furry little animal. Another receiver, recalling an encounter with a mad animal, might feel anger and fear. Still another might think of the person he or she went out with the other night! In other words, meanings are already in people, and the sender is only making "signs" which pull them out. And the sender will never know what the receiver understood from the sign unless there is an opportunity for feedback.

Also in the channel between the sender and receiver, there is distraction. Distraction can be anything from loud noise to competing messages. And it can also be the consequence of the channel itself being complicated. For example, if the channel between speaker and audience is the air between them, then any distraction could be something like the noise made by other members of the audience or the temperature of the room or the lighting. But if the channel is a television camera with all the technology between camera and receiver, the distraction factor becomes more complicated. This is especially true because the sender has no indication of audience response. At least the speaker in the room can see the audience and its body language.

Feedback then becomes critical for clarity in communication. In fact, some researchers believe that less than half of a message is understood the first time it is sent. And because receivers select the parts of the message received, the sender never knows what got through. A mass medium generally provides no feedback, and what feedback it does provide is not immediate or reliably effective. In the world of new technology, marketers are rethinking how and when they use newspapers and television. The whole business of media relations is taking on a different look, while public speeches, special events, personal visits, e-mail, chat rooms, e-surveys, and the whole Internet world take on new significance. This is because they all provide feedback and the potential for interaction. (Even though direct mail has little immediate feedback, it does permit market segmentation, so that messages can be better tailored for the receiver.)

In light of all this, research tells us that four conditions are necessary for communication effectiveness:

1. Get their attention.
2. Keep messages simple.
3. Make sure to seek feedback.
4. Repeat, repeat, repeat.

Also take into account the natural qualities of each medium as it has evolved through communication revolutions and their impact on each audience segment.

KEY INSIGHTS FROM RESEARCH

People retain very little. This is discouraging since the more we tell people about our institutions, the less they seem to know. We struggle and struggle to tell them facts and stories only to find out that, even if they read what we send them, they retain very little. As mentioned above, most think people retain 50 percent or less of a single communication. What does this mean to our work?

First, it means that we need to concentrate on communicating only a very few messages and to keep our stories simple and direct. While it is frustrating that people remember so little, we can use what we know about communication to improve the odds.

Second, we can establish editorial policies to select subject matter, stories, and events that reinforce one of the institution's identity-shaping message points to write stories about. That way, even if they don't remember the specific story or fact over time, they will come to have a better understanding of the institution's uniqueness. They will eventually remember reinforced messages.

The more we tell people about our institutions, the less they seem to know.

Third, realize that overall attitude and enthusiasm is formed over time as a collective impression from many communications—and this is ultimately what you want to happen. Some people will connect to specific stories, but those who don't may still develop positive attitudes along with a sense of "I know what this place is about."

Strategic thinking, then, helps us focus on what can be accomplished, rather than just sending things out and ignoring the fact that results are poor. Draw a pyramid with your name at the top and the message points lined up below it; then choose the stories to communicate based on their capacity to clarify points.

People hear what they want. If a person has made up his or her mind on a particular topic, anything you say in the short term will serve only to reinforce what they already believe. A good speech by a Democrat will make good Republicans better Republicans every time. This is a frustrating truth about communication. Changing minds is possible only if you make an effort to do it. And it won't happen through the mass media; it will only happen through direct and interactive communication.

The strategic model for changing minds has three steps. First, open up your audience's mind. Your first effort is to raise questions and challenge them with new ideas without presenting any conclusions. Your objective is to open up minds, not to directly confront or challenge them with another point of view. A direct challenge always produces a defensive response. Second, present a variety of new points of view. Point out that there are many right answers to most questions, and that there are a number of possibilities here. Third, gradually move them to the conclusion you prefer. Even this does not always work. But the dialogue, if handled well, can increase respect for your point of view and, with regard to an institution, increase overall appreciation of what it stands for.

Media sets the agenda. What is often referred to as the "agenda theory" means that mass media is far more effective at determining *what* you think about than determining your opinion about it. If it's in the news, it's important and visible. But your friends and colleagues will have greater influence on your opinions. These are your opinion leaders, and they are very important in the communication process.

Strategic thinking helps you understand that your primary mass-media objective is to be visible and to have positive feelings attached to the way you are reported. As long as it is not scandalous, it really does not matter what the story is—and no one is likely to remember the story for very long anyway. And if you can define your market segments narrowly enough, you may not even need mass-media exposure to be visible to your constituency. Once you establish name visibility, you can aim direct communication to opinion leaders in each market segment who will influence how the others think.

Inoculation can work. One important truth of communication is that when someone poses a challenging question or makes a direct remark, the person who receives it is from that moment on in a defensive position. This is very important in media relations, especially in times of crisis. By making the first statement, you establish your authority and from then on can answer questions from a position of strength.

Strategic thinking leads you to brainstorm all of those topics that you might want to "inoculate." Choose issues and subjects you might want to communicate, so later you do not wind up in a negative role.

People choose poor communication. This idea relates more to internal communication, but it can apply to other situations too. People tend to protect themselves on some topics and in some situations, or they imply criticism of someone by saying, "I was never told that." This can happen even when they knew it all along, and it usually means they heard it but they didn't hear it the way they wanted to hear it. The strategic solution to this is perseverance and knowing that this is common behavior. Communication is a process, and it does take time.

Rumors are natural. As mentioned before, people retain half or less of a given communication. Retelling a story often launches a rumor. Rumors have three stages. The first, *leveling*, occurs when selective perception causes the receiver to ignore portions of the message. The second step, *sharpening*, is the result of leveling and means the remaining part of the message receives more importance than the sender intended. The third step, *creative embedding*, happens when the receiver adds new material to the message when it is sent again. The receiver usually thinks that this makes the message clearer, but as messages are told and retold the meaning changes completely.

Sometimes rumors are started with hostile intent. But most times messages that are important and to some degree ambiguous end up as rumors, a natural process that becomes a problem for organizational communicators and marketers. The strategic response is to clarify and simplify the original message and repeat it again and again directly to specific targeted audiences.

Strategic communication involves taking the time and making the effort to apply what we know about the way communication works. It is also a way of thinking. What is our objective? What is our target market? Is our message simple enough? What media are the best in this case? What are their natural characteristics? Can I combine several of them to maximize effectiveness? Where can I build in feedback? How will I respond? How often and in what ways can I repeat this message?

In the final analysis, your aim is to achieve visibility for your institution within target-market segments and to be received in a positive context. You want your prospects to know as much about you as possible. But assuming that their knowledge will be limited, you want them to at least have a positive attitude. You are functioning in a communication-cluttered environment, and ignoring these suggestions means you will only contribute to the clutter.

CHAPTER FIVE

Organizing for Effective Marketing

Our objective is to adapt the latest thinking about integrated and relationship marketing to the academy in order to enhance competitiveness and organizational effectiveness, especially as they relate to visibility, admissions, fund raising, alumni relations, curriculum planning, student-program planning, athletics, and overall morale. The organizational challenge is that many of these areas report to different administrative officers who have traditionally operated independent from each other.

The central idea behind integrated marketing is that if all these areas coordinated their thinking and planning around a clearly defined mission and set of goals, they could accomplish much more with already existing human and financial resources. And if this is true, imagine what they could accomplish if the resulting organizational synergy attracted new resources. Indeed, success breeds success, even in marketing. When people in an institution become proud of the way the institution is being shaped and communicated, they find new resources to do more of both.

A TASK FORCE OR RESTRUCTURE?

Historically, academic institutions maintain decentralized marketing and communication functions that report to different officers and units. Admissions and continuing education usually report to the chief academic officer. Public relations, publications, alumni affairs, and fund raising report to the chief advancement officer. The athletics director may report anywhere, including directly to the president. The campus police can report many different places as well. The bookstore and human resources report to the chief business officer. All student programs report to the chief student affairs officer. And all of these either are or have marketing functions or influence.

What is the best way to organize them?

Some argue for creating a marketing division to bring more of these units together. Most institutions with experience do eventually over time somewhat change their structure to make their operations more efficient. Even then it is impossible to put all of the units in one division that will need to work together more closely if a true integration of marketing is to succeed. Teams that cross unit lines will always be necessary.

Begin with a task-force approach, and let restructuring emerge over time. Experience teaches that restructuring is a very institution-specific matter, and that all kinds of approaches will work—depending (as I noted before) on historical conventions and management styles. In some cases, very traditional models can stay in place while the task force does the job. In other cases, some creative change that liberates people and ideas might be very healthy.

ORCHESTRATING THE INSTITUTION

Some have compared the task of integrating marketing to conducting an orchestra. The analogy may have some holes, but it is helpful nonetheless. Someone has to be the composer, the person who sees how a scenario can be charted and puts all of that together. Someone has to gather the players, rehearse them, and manage their performance. In the academy, this might be two people: the president, who is the ultimate leader, and the person who chairs the effort and works with the performers. Each section of performers has an important role to play. Each section is more prominent at some times than others. Some musicians are soloists, while others provide support and foundation. But together they make beautiful music.

I like this analogy because I believe that there is a kind of magic in group synergy. When it comes to marketing and communications, the sum is greater than its parts. And like singing in a choir, no thrill is greater than being in the middle of the process and having a chance to feel the moment when the dramatic climax is reached. It's satisfying for the soloists, but it's just as satisfying for the all the other musicians.

MOBILIZING TALENT AND RESOURCES

Integrated marketing clearly makes use of resources more effectively. Many times professionals in one unit will feel that they cannot accomplish another thing without more staff, that there are just not enough people to get the job done. When it is possible to search institution-wide for marketing and communication talent, however, it soon becomes clear that even small places have more talent than you thought.

Also, there is usually more money around than you thought. Units protect their budgets, but when the president announces the launching of an integrated approach to marketing and that everyone is expected to cooperate, the walls begin to crack a little. But the breakthrough only comes over time, when the group has gotten to know and respect each other and has had time to develop goals and initiatives together. Then a miracle occurs. People gradually begin to combine resources, human and financial, to move ahead projects they deem important.

THE POWER OF TEAMWORK

For those not used to it, learning to work in teams takes a little time. The fear, of course, is that individual creativity and achievement will be clouded by the crowd and that less-worthy team members will end up getting too much credit. But it really doesn't work out that way. Like the Pandora's box argument against asking people for ideas, experience teaches that the opposite actually occurs. Conventional wisdom is wrong again. All team members do experience the thrill of victory—that is true—but after a successful project, team members are the ones who insist on celebrating the individual achievers who made the real difference. Individual achievers actually get more out of working with creative teams than working alone.

But teams are most helpful in dealing with the failures. When a team fails, individuals are spared immediate blame, and the group pulls together to figure out what went wrong. And a group that has been working together can generate new ideas faster and turn the problem around better than an individual can. Having teams used to working together is most appreciated during the low points. And when teams have members from many units in the institution, the capacity to pull together in a crisis is most comforting.

Team members share risks, which is both good and bad. The bad part is that an inexperienced team might assume too big a risk because no individual feels individually threatened. But it doesn't take long for a group to realize that danger and to continually remind itself of it. The good part, however, is that a group has more creative courage than most individuals and can generate more excitement while it moves the institution ahead. Experience teaches that failures are few and damage doesn't last. And, of course, the absolute necessary byproduct of the team approach is getting everyone on the same page with respect to message and competitive advantage.

FINDING A MARKETING CHAMPION

The question of who serves as point person in an integrated marketing program is critical. In some institutions, the individual may be hard to find. Here are some of the necessary qualities.

The marketing champion must first and foremost understand the subject matter. Many people currently working in public relations, fund raising, and admissions do not sufficiently understand marketing. And if they do not understand the difference when they move into marketing, they will continue to operate from their previous perspectives and priorities. However, more and more people coming from these areas are gaining the necessary knowledge and broader perspective to do the job. Also, some faculty members with marketing backgrounds have interest in higher-education marketing. And there may be people in various other positions with marketing backgrounds and interests. Don't overlook people in continuing education, a special area of higher education where marketing skills have been important for years. It's critical to find one of these people in your institution or elsewhere.

The marketing champion must first and foremost understand the subject matter.

Next, the champion needs to be a process person. He or she needs to appreciate teamwork and have strong facilitation skills. Much of the work will involve bringing talented people together, inspiring them to perform, and dealing with conflicts as they develop. This is not a top-down management situation. It is one that requires diplomacy, savvy, and the ability to negotiate with a whole array of individuals and groups.

That brings us to determination. This is not an easy task. There are roadblocks and barriers. Some will be past practices, and others will be individual people. Still others will be attitudes and fears. Persistence will be required, and the champion will experience a good deal of loneliness on the road ahead.

Credibility is also important, and gaining it with all of the disparate groups on campus will be a challenge. The person has to have appropriate marketing background credentials and experience and yet have credibility with faculty. Career academics may need to be convinced, and this can happen only when someone they trust leads the way.

All these qualities are hard to find in one person, but it is imperative to do so. Some institutions might want to begin early by sending people with potential to conferences and seminars. Also, when you travel, keep an eye out for people emerging in the field. As time goes by, more people will be available. The interest in the field is gaining momentum. Indeed, in March 2001 *Smart Money* magazine listed marketing as the hottest career opportunity in higher education.

THE ROLE OF EXECUTIVE COMMUNICATION

An integrated marketing initiative will not get very far without presidential leadership and cooperation from the executive cabinet. It is a total institutional enterprise that works when top leadership is not only on board, but when they are leading the way.

If the task-force approach is chosen, the president should send a letter of appointment to its members. He or she should conduct the first meeting, during which the challenge is made, the champion introduced, and support is pledged. It is wise for the president to realistically define what "support" means. It is fine to suggest that the first task is to look for ways to get more out of existing resources. It is also important to be able to say that, over time, as plans become more clear, the institution will make every effort to find ways, through budgeting and/or fund raising, to support new initiatives. But it is important and acceptable to be realistic with respect to setting expectations. Teams will accept parameters as long as they see where and how progress can be made.

The president should be prepared to occasionally attend task-force meetings to hear progress reports and answer questions. The entire process should be shaped as a project of the president's office, with the task force reporting directly to it. Cabinet members should be asked to inform staff members about the importance of complete cooperation for moving the institution ahead. This is critical because even though this is a presidential project, some line managers may be concerned with how "the boss" is reacting to this potential invasion of territory. The president and vice presidents need to make it clear that this cooperation is not at all a territorial issue.

DEALING WITH THE BARRIERS

What hurdles need to be jumped to enhance the marketing of academic institutions? The process resembles a train moving out from the station. Some board the train early, others jump on as it pulls away from the station, others stand on the platform and wave, and still others don't even come to the station. The objective can never be to win everyone over to the cause—which can be very frustrating because it won't happen. But many people with reservations and sincere concerns can and will eventually cooperate when they see that the objective is to improve, not cheapen, the academy.

A misunderstanding of the word "marketing." Many academics equate marketing to selling shoes and are offended by the whole idea of marketing educational institutions. They think marketing means appealing to students by just giving them what they want. We have discussed how marketing establishes contact based on needs and provides the information necessary to develop products and programs that exceed expectations. We have also discussed how, as a way of thinking, marketing is actually about achieving greater excellence and building a better academic reputation. Most skeptics will over time come to see this, but those championing this new cause will have to look for and take every opportunity to explain it. Meeting with the faculty senate, fielding questions in staff meetings, and including key faculty members in the process are all critical. Patience and persistence are required.

Some unit heads will consider integrated marketing and the use of teams that cross unit boundaries a challenge to their autonomy and territory.

Threatened line managers. Some unit heads will consider integrated marketing and the use of teams that cross unit boundaries a challenge to their autonomy and territory. Admissions deans, for example, may find the idea of all of these outside people telling them what to do to be unacceptable. They prefer to be given the goal and then left alone to determine how to meet it. The problem here is that not enough of the resources of the institution are being used, and that by involving public relations, alumni relations, the bookstore manager, key faculty members, and others, so much more can be achieved.

Unit heads should be told that the integrated process is intended mostly to generate new initiatives that can be added on top of their daily work to improve the intensity of their impact. Furthermore, if they find any initiative that directly affects their operation to be unacceptable, they can veto it. This usually alleviates their fears, and in practice few vetoes are exercised because it quickly becomes obvious that this process produces far more benefit to all than harm to the few.

The devil's advocate. Every institution has devil's advocates, and at least one winds up on every task force. They can be useful in making sure every objection is appropriately dealt with, but, if they become obstructionists in meetings, they must be dealt with individually outside meeting time. Do not become obsessed with changing their behavior. They will not change. Your objective is to contain them, to keep them from wasting the group's time. Put them on the agenda to speak from time to time, schedule and limit the amount of time to discuss, and then move on. If not contained in this manner, the devil's advocate can lob an off-the-agenda idea bomb into the middle of a discussion that sidetracks the group for hours.

Let them speak, limit discussion to a specific time, and move on—remembering all the time that you will not change them and that it really is better to have them inside the tent with you instead of outside starting rumors and making trouble.

TASK FORCE MEMBERSHIP

Determining who serves on the task force is one of the most important decisions of the entire project. The task force should include all of the people talented with respect to marketing and communication no matter where they are. All relevant units must be represented, yet the group should not be too big to function. Areas to consider include:

- Admissions
- Marketing
- Financial aid
- Public relations
- Publications writing
- Graphic design
- Student programming
- Bookstore
- Academic administration
- Faculty leadership
- Athletics
- Fund raising
- Alumni relations

- Continuing education
- Security
- Marketing faculty
- Trustees
- Marketing communications

Eighteen or more—plus the chair and president—make for too large a group to handle many creative tasks. You either have to be more selective or build a more elaborate process to involve them all. One approach is to establish a three-tier organization. The largest group is the *steering group*, which meets monthly at the beginning and several times a year thereafter. Members discuss their overall impressions of how things are going, set broad goals, hear reports as appropriate, and take a strong role in getting others in the institution to feel connected to the process. A smaller *planning group* sets objectives to achieve the goals and to commission appropriate research projects. This is a lean and mean group of key marketing professionals. *Action groups* are then formed to plan and carry out specific initiatives.

The action groups include some members from the task force, but others can be added as appropriate. These groups need to be small but include the right people to carry out projects. For example, most will need a strategic thinker, a writer, a designer, and other experts in the area under consideration. Action groups can be formed to add marketing intensity to admissions, visibility, internal relations, alumni relations, athletics, to name a few. Not too many action groups should be named at first. Set a few doable goals, and form action groups for each of these.

ACHIEVING DOABLE GOALS

The first task of the task force will be to set some achievable goals. This is best accomplished in a retreat setting where members can take time to get to know each other, answer everyone's questions, and come to understand the subject matter as well as set goals. Here is where you can review and discuss the subject matter of this book.

Usually, the primary reason for initiating an integrated marketing effort at this particular time in the institution's history dictates the primary goal. There are a number of possible reasons: The institution may be suffering a decline in enrollment, the most compelling reason for most people. The institution may not be in a decline, but it is aware of the competition out there and wants to get ahead of the game. The institution may be considering a fund-raising campaign; it is aware of competition from other campaigns and therefore wants to intensify its relationship-building activities. Or current leadership may feel the need for a renewal initiative because a recent survey uncovered some dissatisfaction and a growing sense of plateau. Or a new president may be looking for a bold project to establish themes and goals for a new administration. There are many possible hooks for launching integrated marketing, but it's important to identify the main one as a guide for setting some basic goals.

Frankly, the two most common initial goals are to increase the number of undergraduate applications and increase visibility. These are good places to start because you can make tangible improvements by making better use of existing resources. Other goals will eventually appear, some related to general university needs and others related to specific programs. The most typical goals include:

- Broader alumni participation
- Deeper donor commitment
- Expanded continuing-education enrollment
- More MBA students
- More Ph.D. students
- Better internal communication
- Higher attendance at events—athletics, fine arts, lectures

Eventually, the discussion will lead to a consideration of all aspects of marketing, not only what you can accomplish through better marketing communications. Price, and learning environments and methods, and academic and student programs will come up. If some of the right people are present at this time, a whole new approach to overall institutional strategic planning will have been enabled. But that's a subject for a later chapter.

A PLAN OR A BLUEPRINT?

Developing a plan of any sort meets resistance in any organization. That is because most people have experience with long, complicated projects that have produced hundreds of pages that wind up sitting on a shelf. Most marketing textbooks teach you to develop written plans that can do just that. When who-does-what-by-when becomes too rigidly prescribed, the plan itself cannot be implemented. The creative dynamic spirit is lost, which is deadly for fundamentally creative people.

This dysfunction cannot happen here because the process never ends. Ideas come in all the time, and new information and creative suggestions modify activities on a daily basis. That is what is so exciting about the integrated approach. No one can ever say, "You didn't ask me." Any good idea can elicit an instant response. It is truly a permanent, ongoing, never-ending planning, implementing and evaluating activity.

Therefore, consider a blueprint approach with different layers of specificity. The main blueprint includes mission, vision, values, overall goals, central message and themes, and the primary initiatives necessary to achieve those goals. (See Appendix C.) That's enough to guide operations, and it can be readily remembered. Action groups and support offices can add the who-does-what-by-when to their operating plan, understanding that this changes as needed. The blueprint then is updated at least quarterly and used as an outline to keep others informed and to make progress reports. Bottom line: Integrated marking, once organized and implemented, is an ongoing self-correcting process.

INVOLVEMENT OF TRUSTEES AND OUTSIDE EXPERTS

Some fear that involving trustees invites inappropriate micromanagement. Experience again teaches otherwise. As in fund raising, trustees have a keen interest in marketing and can bring expertise and resources to the table. The key is to select the right ones, and, if you have not done this before, you might not have the right ones readily at hand. The right trustee who loves the institution and has a depth of experience with marketing can be very constructive and helpful. You need not be concerned that trustees will be too unrealistic for the academy if you take care to involve them in the whole process.

Outside professionals can actually be more of a challenge than trustees. They are more likely to jump to the conclusion that the academy needs their help and come forth too quickly with awkward and unworkable ideas. But when these practitioners do take the time to get their minds engaged with a whole new industry and kind of marketing, they end up contributing immeasurably. It's critical to take the time to make all of these selections very carefully—not to eliminate those who would challenge you, but rather to eliminate those who will waste your time.

In the final analysis, participation in a project like this is truly a challenge worth taking. There are hurdles to jump, but the rewards are great. It's a matter of taking a truly beautiful and wonderful institution, establishing a process that in time will make it even better, and then getting people to know, appreciate, and support it as they never have before. And to accomplish all this in an information-cluttered, highly competitive world.

CHAPTER SIX

Does Size Matter?
How Marketing Works in Different Settings

Visits to more than 25 campuses of all sizes and categories around the world reveal that the application of marketing thinking to advancement is a very institution-specific matter. Each institution has a different history, a special culture, its own management philosophy, unique programs, specific strengths, compelling creative opportunities, and diverse talents to call upon. While this is true regardless of the size of the institution, size and type do make some difference. From a marketing perspective, there are at least five categories to consider: small colleges, medium-sized universities, regional public institutions, large public/state universities, independent primary, middle, and secondary schools.

SMALL COLLEGES

In a competitive marketplace, small colleges offer the greatest risk and the most exciting opportunities. But in this overly aggressive environment, any small school that fails to take specific steps to secure a place for itself will eventually get squeezed out of the picture. Indeed, in the coming decade, more and more small colleges are likely to fail.

A small college that sits back and waits for students and donors to come can fall way behind very quickly or even have to close its doors. One small college in Oklahoma closed in 2001 because it waited too long to step out. When it finally did take action, the market did not respond quickly enough to save it. It was located in a small town far from high population centers and faced severe competition from popular larger public universities. Most students come from within a few hundred miles of an institution, but this institution did not develop this market well enough. A church-related institution, it was unable to make that association compelling enough to attract students from greater distances. In the final analysis, its decline had begun years before, and efforts to revitalize it were at first too weak and in the end too late.

It's easy for small colleges to decide that their size and limited resources are extreme liabilities. After all, how can they afford to compete with larger, wealthier institutions? It's the same for small businesses versus larger corporations. If a small business goes head-to-head with a large corporation, it can fail. But if it finds its own special niche and builds loyal relationships, it will thrive. The key is for the small college to carve out its own market segments and become so effective at serving them that they virtually own them.

Small colleges have a real opportunity to thrive. It isn't the amount of money they can spend. It's how compelling they can make their competitive advantages and how effectively they identify specific marketing segments narrow enough to fit their resource capability. They should not worry about getting into the *New York Times*, but rather they should worry about building relationships within markets narrowly defined both geographically and demographically.

It takes both an entrepreneurial president and an integrated marketing task force. The president should be entrepreneurial in the educational sense. He or she must have ideas, be able to articulate them, and thereby generate excitement about stepping out with a distinction. The task force can get everyone on the same page and, of course, consultants are available to provide outside perspective and advice.

One women's college in New England (names of universities are not used in this book for proprietary reasons) is developing a niche around the attitude it seeks in the woman it recruits, which matches the attitude possessed by most of its graduates over the years. It recruits internationally for women who are aggressive, who want to position themselves on the edge, and who will be able, if they choose, to compete in a somewhat male-dominated world.

Several small colleges in New England and the Southeast stress the discipline of a military heritage; another in the Southwest bases its education around a basic set of readings; an institution in California exposes all students to creative development through the arts; and many more have their own special identities. Small colleges with exciting leadership, a clear mission that can define a niche, clearly focused target markets, and a capacity to mobilize its people inside and out will have grand futures in these exciting times. Also, small colleges in general have the appealing advantages of apparently safe campuses, professors who mentor students, communities that support whole-person growth and development, and a tradition of faculty and staff working together as a team. Small colleges will probably end up allocating more resources to marketing than in the past, but success is affordable if the project is shaped properly and the president leads the way.

MEDIUM-SIZED UNIVERSITIES

While most medium-sized schools are not at risk, many face the real potential of decline when competition heats up. As the competitive market brings more choices and new competitors into the picture (such as for-profit universities), the market for medium-sized universities may actually shrink. For many, the main competition will be regional publics that claim the advantages of a private for the price of a public. The main challenge for medium-sized universities will be delivering on their promises.

The problem with marketing is not that it cheapens the academy, but that as sophisticated consumers search for genuine quality it often reveals the school's weaknesses. These schools can meet the challenge because many of them are still small enough to orchestrate a total response. But it is a formidable task that requires very strong leadership.

Even top-tier schools should improve their approach to marketing because over time their domination will fade. Marketplaces change, as do trends. And as more products and services come to market, more hot brands appear. Witness the American automobile industry. Lexus wasn't even a factor in Lincoln's world a number of years ago. And just as the foreign market changed the whole automobile market, so will it change higher education.

As increased foreign competition changes the higher education marketplace and second-tier U.S. schools step out more aggressively, more and more of the very top students and their savvy parents will exploit their negotiation positions. All of these alternative schools will be shaping programs that will attract more top students, give them prestige while on campus, and guarantee them very good careers.

Mid-sized schools, like small colleges, have real potential to thrive with integrated marketing, and it should be especially attractive to schools below the top tier. Here is where defining a compelling institutional competitive advantage and finding niches for specific programs can have the biggest impact. But the larger the setting, the more complicated the task. Again, strong leadership is required as well as the perseverance to work through the barriers and issues described in other chapters.

Several medium-sized colleges are defining core curricula that they hope will become attractive competitive advantages. Several are building basic offerings for all students, regardless of their major concentration, around the theme of leadership. Several put emphasis on "technology for all" out front. And of course, many church-related institutions seek to clarify what church affiliation really means with respect to the student experience. One medium-sized university in central Texas simultaneously raised its price significantly, announced a new core curriculum based on the great books, and promised to move to a significantly new level of recognition in the coming years.

The first task for these universities is to decide whether they hope to move up on the big list of all universities or to establish an industry category in which they can be number one or two. This is a critical early decision because it determines how they use the benchmarking information they gather in marketing research. Is the school trying to become more similar to or more different from its aspirant schools? Each situation presents a distinct set of challenges and opportunities, but in every case integrated marketing can play a major role in clarifying the institution's identity and making it more competitive.

REGIONAL PUBLIC INSTITUTIONS

These institutions have a very high potential to become more competitive by utilizing integrated marketing. As mentioned above, many will claim to offer the advantages of a private at the price of a public. And there will probably be a growing market for that kind of institution.

Besides price, one advantage of a public is its convenience. More and more students are choosing to attend colleges and universities closer to home, and schools that combine price with convenience have a genuine appeal. The residential opportunities in most of these institutions give students the feeling of going away to school. This is also appealing for Hispanic and other minority populations where strong family values encourage students to remain closer to home.

The biggest issue for some regional publics is quality, a problem that is sometimes real and sometimes only a matter of perception. Marketing analysis, however, will often reveal weaknesses in programs and student services that need to be addressed. The biggest challenge is to make certain that promises can be delivered on. Having said that, strong leadership combined with all the other tools of integrated marketing can bring these regional campuses into their own.

One regional public university in Utah has done a particularly good job of realizing its marketing potential. It has focused on showing how its separate schools and colleges provide solid private-university-type benefits, and it has used institutional slogans to create a total, single institutional identity. Shaping a clear and distinct overall institutional identity might be the biggest marketing challenge for any diverse public university, and regionals are the best positioned to accomplish it.

Two regional universities in Canada face a similar problem. Economic issues have caused an overall population decline, which causes a decline in enrollment, which means a decline in government support as well. The challenge, then, is to attract a higher proportion of those remaining in the province, or to attract more students from other provinces, or to take a unique leadership role in developing the overall economy, or to do all of the above. The integrated marketing approach, with its appropriate mobilization of talents, can help with any or all these.

The biggest issue for some regional publics is quality, a problem that is sometimes real and sometimes only a matter of perception.

The idea of a university leading a future-planning project for a region is particularly intriguing, and it could very well be a marketing idea for others in similar circumstances. This idea could apply to a county, state, city, or any region in the world. It is marketing because it builds bonded relationships with all of the opinion leaders who can attract students and money to your institution. And such a project leaves an institution with higher visibility, a better reputation, and significantly more prestige. The whole institution seems relevant to what is going on around it.

Universities with more than one campus have separate regional identities at separate campus locations. Instead of being perceived as one university, the public really sees it as two that almost have to be marketed as two different places. One regional public in Canada with this problem is uncertain as to how to solve it. It can try to market each campus separately by giving each one a clearly defined sub-brand and then tying them together with a unified slogan and name. Or it can make the very difficult political decision to become two separate institutions. A lot will depend on just how different the two places are and how graduates of each view their loyalties and preferences. At any rate, the analytical discipline of integrated marketing and market-segment research can help resolve the matter.

One regional public institution in the Southwest discovered a new target market nearby in a neighboring state. In the past, it mainly served rural communities around its own state. But marketing analysis revealed that there was a dense population of potential students in a neighboring state who might appreciate a regional low-cost public with the advantages of a private. What made it even more appealing is that it fit within the trend of students going to school closer to home. To be successful, this school needs to generate the impression that it's stepping out under dynamic leadership and using the mobilization tools of integrated marketing.

LARGE PUBLIC/STATE UNIVERSITIES

The larger the institution, the harder it is to establish a single, unique identity. In fact, most of these institutions won't achieve that status, but integrated marketing can be helpful to them in other ways.

Large public institutions can use the integrated marketing task force concept to mobilize and coordinate talent on a system-wide basis to strengthen cooperation and to share ideas and expertise. Sometimes it can produce agreed-upon slogans and themes that give the total institution a stronger identity. But this can be difficult to accomplish and requires an effective and energetic champion.

Certainly, at the campus and school and college level, integrated marketing can help. At this level the task is very similar to a smaller college or a regional university, and getting down to this level to shape competitive advantage may be a wise marketing strategy for some schools. Of course, the power of the brand name and related prestige of some public institutions will help them overcome other weaknesses, such as being large, impersonal, and confusing to live in. Many larger institutions may be able to promote themselves as a collection of smaller communities.

One very large institution made an effort to introduce integrated marketing but had to severely modify its expectations. It turned out that the long history of individual schools and colleges operating independently frustrated attempts to integrate their efforts—at least at the time. Efforts at greater cooperation in shaping the president's public-appearance agenda and setting a public-relations agenda is what integration has come to mean.

While I have not used names of universities in this book for proprietary reasons, I will make an exception for Texas A&M University, a huge state institution with a clear identity and strong bonded and powerful relationships. A state and regional political power, Texas A&M provides associated advantages for its graduates. Just as Ted Turner was once quoted on a poster saying, "I was cable before cable was cool," the Aggies were integrating before integrating was cool. A massive university with a military-related heritage, Texas A&M has established a single we-stick-together core-related identity that attracts many more applications than it can accept—in recent years from women as well as men. The full-color picture of the school ring at the front of the A&M student-recruiting brochure promotes the desire to earn the honor of wearing it, a powerful and effective appeal. Aggie culture and traditions are integrated throughout all operations, from the smallest academic department to the vast and pervasive worldwide alumni association. Obviously every huge institution cannot do this, but Texas A&M proves that where the founding mission is strong and distinct enough, and the leadership is determined enough, it is indeed possible. And it is done by mobilizing the troops and supporting them with integrated marketing.

INDEPENDENT PRIMARY, MIDDLE, AND SECONDARY SCHOOLS

The independent school world, too, is becoming interested in marketing, the result of observing a change in the marketplace and detecting the need to clarify benefits to increasingly sophisticated consumers. As more and more independent schools improve their marketing and communication, others feel the pressure to do the same.

Independent schools have the same challenges and opportunities as private colleges. They have small marketing-related staffs (or no staff at all), and they have very few resources to commit to the task. But they have one very big advantage. In most independent schools, the faculty and staff work together as a very close team to plan a truly special curriculum and total school experience that appeals to both students and parents. Their challenge is to state this advantage in terms of clearly defined themes and to aggressively tell the story to the people in the community most likely to respond. This is a challenge well suited to integrated marketing.

In addition to establishing a task force, it is often wise for independent schools to bring together admissions, media relations, community relations, parent relations, alumni relations, and fund raising into one division. This is helpful because there are so few people doing these jobs and because reputation building and student recruiting can take place largely through these channels. It is critical that the school is visible and impressive to community leaders, but visibility is not necessary beyond these market segments. News media presence is not as important as sometimes thought. Lots of time can be wasted trying to get a non-news story into the newspaper when communicating directly with opinion leaders is so much more effective.

In the case of boarding schools, marketing planning and strategies should be planned and dealt with separately from the local commuter students. Here, too, parents, alumni, donors, and the organizations that sent students in the past are the most likely key targets for personal references. This will remain the most effective marketing strategy. A really imaginative program or project may attract national media attention, but attaining reputation through the national media story is not likely to happen. Direct communication with target markets remains most cost effective. Taking an integrated approach in independent schools means coordinating the total team in order to build relationships with the opinion leaders in targeted markets—parents, alumni, donors, and community leaders.

CHAPTER SEVEN

Cost-effective Market Research

For a marketing program to be effective, it must have ongoing research activity. That is the only way to achieve and maintain a workable understanding of the marketplace in a climate that is changing almost on a daily basis. It really is the only way to find out what people are thinking and to spot trends as they develop.

Because most institutions have made no provisions in their budgets for research, this may be the most difficult part of launching a new marketing program. If you need resources to get started, or if you need to make difficult decisions about reallocating some money, supporting some initial research is the most likely area. This is really ironic when you think about it. Most institutions teach the importance of investigation and research, and many are fundamentally research institutions, but few perform research to understand their own business and marketplace.

RESEARCH BY MARKET SEGMENT

Some of the reluctance to perform market research is due to poor past experience. Typically, someone some time in the past made the case for a very expensive comprehensive image study. The institution bit the bullet and did the study only to receive pages and pages of results that were interesting but not all that helpful. Most people felt that the study only confirmed what they already knew, and no one thought that it was worth the time, effort, and money. A lot of people on campus worked very hard to think of everything they ever wanted to know, and expensive outside experts constructed a vast questionnaire that explored virtually every concern.

That was the problem. The study was too complicated and too comprehensive. It tried to do too much and ended up producing interesting reading with no guidance for action. And it produced a huge report that, because of its volume, really couldn't be used to guide decisions. It went into a file with everyone feeling, "We won't do that again."

The rule of thumb is to focus on one market segment at a time and keep the list of questions as short as possible. Ask only the questions that will inform action, and resist the temptation to think, "Wouldn't it be nice to know this or that?" Instead, think only, "What decision am I trying to make here, and what do I really need to know in order to make it?" When you focus on one specific market segment and clarify what you really need to know, research projects become smaller and therefore cheaper, and you get information you actually can use.

TYPES OF RESEARCH

Image Research

Image research usually measures awareness, attitude, and knowledge. Have they heard of you? What do they think of you? What do they know about you? Finding out what they know about you will be very discouraging. Even your closest supporters will actually know very little about your programs and opportunities. And what they think they know will often be naïve or downright wrong. You will feel you have spent years sending out newsletters, magazines, and countless brochures and news releases only to learn you have failed dismally. These people know nothing.

Don't feel too badly. Truthfully, *knowledge* is the least important category of the three. If you have been successful, they will at least be aware of you and like you—and those should be your primary objectives. Achieving those two objectives builds a feeling of relationship that encourages them to help you find students and raise money. And it establishes the climate for word-of-mouth support that builds reputation and expands awareness.

Remember how the communications process works. People forget at least half the message immediately, and over time they forget even more. But opinion leaders who become stakeholders in one way or another become knowledgeable in ways meaningful to them. They are not going to know what you think they should know. In fact, this also is true of the education your graduates received at your institution!

Awareness is very important. More and more educational marketers concede that the more someone hears about your institution the more important they think it is. That means that getting the name established within target market segments is one of the most important things you can do, and why the subject of branding (see Chapter 11) has lately taken on more importance in academic marketing.

Attitude is important too, but a positive attitude will usually follow from awareness and continued communication. Of course, attitude is complicated by whether you are asking about feelings in isolation from or in relation to your competitors. It's interesting to know both, but more direct and intense communications will usually improve attitude either way.

The ultimate objective of image research is to define the scope and shape of your problem. If no one has heard of you in your target market, you have a lot of basic work to do. If they are aware of you and put you above your competitors, you are in great shape. If you fall below your competitors, it generally means that allegiances are just stronger elsewhere, or that they are not hearing enough from you, or both. Again, direct and ongoing communication that reinforces your institution's competitive advantage is the answer.

Communications Audits

One of the most important initial exercises is a communication audit. Your objective is to analyze all of your communications with each market segment for message and design clarity as well as consistency. Begin with your student-recruiting materials because they set the overall institutional identity message and tone for all the rest.

First, collect all of the materials sent to prospective students and lay them out on a table. Include cover letters and anything else that is part of what they receive. Now determine where in the mix they receive phone calls or are likely to make campus visits—and put a piece of paper so noting in the appropriate spot. Each of these papers should also bear a description of the assumed substance of those communications. Now begin what in research terminology is called a content analysis.

Write down exactly what you are looking for so that your evaluation is systematic. First, what is the *central message*, how often does it appear, and what is its level of clarity? Is it up front enough? Is it repeated often enough? Does it come through the collection of materials with enough intensity to establish identity?

Second, is the design consistent? Do the pieces have a family look? While consistency is critical to establishing and maintaining identity, each piece must also have enough distinction to stand out from the clutter. This is the real challenge of graphic design—to make the pieces look like a family and yet be individually distinctive too! Usually, this is the location of the most inconsistency and what makes many feel that these pieces all come from different places.

Third, what is the level of specificity versus simplicity? Is there enough or too much information? Is information presented so that it can be easily found and skimmed? Do the pieces feel well organized?

Fourth, what about timing? Are you communicating with people at the right time and with the right frequency? If not, would sending postcards help you keep connected? Do the phone calls tie in appropriately with information received?

Fifth, what is the overall impact at the end of the process? What is the total impact of the total mix? This is very important. Although each one should establish competitive advantage in its own way with clarity, not every piece should communicate every point. People often criticize a particular communication for what it does not contain when that subject is covered elsewhere more effectively. It is important to evaluate the whole mix and the total impact.

This kind of analysis is also important for all communications going to alumni and donors. It is also important to subject your advertising program, institution-wide, to the same kind of examination. With individual units and the academic departments placing advertising for everything from football camps to music lessons, it is very important to maintain in all of them a consistency of look and competitive advantage message. This is the only way your unique identity will ever be perceived in the marketplace.

Media Preference

It is important to determine which media people prefer for receiving information from you. Major higher education marketing and communication consultant organizations such as Stamats and Lipman Hearne perform generic generation-based studies that focus on the undergraduate student market. It is still important, however, to get your own information from your own markets, as you may find some very interesting clues for new and effective initiatives.

For example, one institution found it effective to mix novelties such as refrigerator magnets and T-shirts with more standard direct-mail materials. Another added a periodic e-mail newsletter that emphasized current on-campus activities to enhance immediacy and give the whole process more of an interactive feeling. Still another institution found occasional humorous postcards an effective way to maintain continuous communication without seeming overbearing. More about media preferences will be discussed in later chapters on student recruiting, branding, and dealing with donors.

Consumer Satisfaction

Few institutions conduct consumer-satisfaction studies. If done at all, it is usually at the time a student chooses to leave. These are called retention studies, and they are usually not very helpful. One problem with retention studies is that once students decide to leave they will say most anything to avoid a difficult conversation. Since there are many legitimate reasons why a student might withdraw or transfer to another institution, you learn little about what they were dissatisfied with while they were at your institution.

Current students, long before they think about leaving, should be asked to rate their satisfaction with classes in general, academic counseling, access to faculty and staff when needed, housing, on-campus food services, exercise facilities, career services, health services, campus security, and social and leadership opportunities. This information is vital to planning programs and services.

Another reason why institutions don't conduct customer-satisfaction studies is because all students will know the survey is being conducted and will therefore want to know the results. So will the student newspaper. All of this might affect the timing of the study, because you will want enough time after the results are in to make some response. Don't let this situation should deter you. Everyone will be glad you cared enough to ask, they will appreciate whatever good comes from it, and they will be more patient about results than you think.

You don't have to make every improvement at once. You merely have to demonstrate that you care and that the place is on the move. So pick what improvements you can make, and be aggressive about communicating that they result from the study.

Customer satisfaction studies are helpful with all target markets. In addition to current students, you might consider surveying active alumni, donors, athletics ticket holders, news media gatekeepers, and anyone else you might regard as a customer or client.

What you want to know is how high you can raise the price before it affects enrollment.

Pricing Elasticity

As discussed previously, this is the most complicated area of academic marketing research. Because the public has such a hard time determining just what a higher education should cost, it is easy just to feel generally that the cost is too high.

What you want to know is how high you can raise the price before it affects enrollment. That is usually determined by asking questions related to how each percentage of price increase will affect behavior. This is not an exact science, and it is important to use a firm that has had some experience in pricing research. Results are usually presented along with error probability. For example, a result might read, "If you raise tuition 10 percent, you should not lose more than 4 percent enrollment." That statement would be made for a whole range of percentage increases.

Some institutions experienced no decline in enrollment the first year of a large, say 15 percent, increase. But they did experience a decrease in the second or third year. And there is always the question, "Can we raise the tuition more for starting freshman than for returning students?" Survey these groups separately. Since this is a complicated problem, some institutions perform pricing surveys every two years. This way they can track the results over time and eventually have their own trend information. Since few institutions have this kind of information, most base pricing decisions on the increase in the standard of living plus a "gut feeling."

Benchmarking

This is an analytical study that relates certain behaviors or practices of competitors or aspirant institutions with those of your institution. You may be interested in student acceptance standards, acceptance timing, financial aid practices, size of staff, size of budget, etc. Information that you could gather and benchmark to your practices is endless.

While benchmarking can be helpful, keep in mind several factors. First, the information you get may not be completely accurate. The hotter the competition, the harder institutions make it to get competitive information. Second, because you can spend lot of time doing this, focus on the information you really need and what you will do with it when you get it. Third, understand why you are doing this. Do you want to become more like these schools? This would mean you are looking for best practices to follow and model. Or are you carving out your own niche? This probably means that you want to differentiate yourself from your competitors and adapt their best practices to your specific situation.

Profiling

Profiling is the practice of listing demographic, geographic, and psychographic information about your current customers and then using available data to determine the zip codes for others who are just like them. The practice can be effective if you want more customers like the ones you already have. Profiling can be performed with current students, alumni, donors, and season-ticket holders. It is a matter of doing the work of organizing the data and then contracting with a company that specializes in compiling the lists necessary to produce the match. There are companies that purchase and own census data, information about bankcard holders, mortgage holders, loan holders, catalog purchasers, etc. All this information and more is available for purchase. Usually these firms are in the commercial direct-marketing business, but several with experience with institutions are emerging.

Data mining is a related activity that uses electronic technology, including the Internet, to search the world for existing information that relates to your marketing issues. People experienced in this technique can find out a lot about specific market segments, competitive and aspirant institutions, and even specific individuals. Since you can spend a lot of time gathering useless information, it is very important to have a clear understanding of what you need to know.

Observing Behavior

The study of behavior, either as directly observed or as reported, is very important because people often say they want something that they may not acquire. This disconnect between what they say and what they do is a huge problem for market research. The broadcasting industry learned long ago that people ask for programs they do not watch. When the surveyor stops them on the street and asks, "What kind of programs would you like to see more of on TV?" many who ask for more good drama and documentaries do not actually watch the dramas and documentaries that are already shown. Many of these people really don't know they are lying. They really believe they want more challenging programs, but when they get home they are tired. They turn on the TV and in their search for what to watch pick *Monday Night Football* or a situation comedy that makes them laugh. Many consumers fool themselves and really do not consciously know in advance what they will do. They think they prefer a small college, but at the last minute pick a big state school because they like the feeling of independence.

Asking people to report their behavior or directly observing it, rather than asking them what they prefer, yields useful information. Knowing where they live and what they eat and so forth helps you connect with them where they are. Of course, as I said before, you will lead them far beyond that with extraordinary programs and services. But at the very start you need to know what they do.

For example, many institutions have found they have more women than men, a trend that seems to be growing. One would think that having more women would, when the word gets out, attract more men. Not so. Why? No one seems to be sure. But you may be able to find the answer by observing what men actually do. College-age men seem to hang around with men and meet women in groups at parties, but they generally want to impress the guys, focus on sports, and be independent. How do we use this knowledge to attract more men?

Evaluating Research

Evaluating the results of marketing is one of our biggest challenges. Of course, if we have students, we are raising money, and fewer and fewer people are complaining about visibility, we are successful. But how do we know what is working and what is not? I will address this separately in Chapter 19.

METHODS OF RESEARCH

Unless you have a trained and experienced person on staff, it is best to work with an outside research firm. There are a number of methods that they might choose to use.

Mail Surveys

The primary advantage of mail surveys is the capacity to reach large numbers of people. The disadvantages are fewer responses, the length of time it takes to do the project, the tendency to get more data than you can use, and the cost. Printing the materials, postage to send and return the survey, and incentives to fill out the questionnaire can become expensive. And more and more people seem to be throwing them away.

Telephone Surveys

Most market surveys are conducted by telephone. The primary limitation is that telephone surveys should be limited to only a few questions. But, as said before, we should discipline ourselves to ask fewer questions for other reasons as well. We should ask only what we absolutely need to know anyway. The advantage of telephone surveys is that once a needed response number is determined statistically, calls can be made until that number is reached. A high level of statistical accuracy is possible and, when focused on a target market and limited in scope, telephone surveys are generally faster and more economical.

E-Surveys

As we obtain reliable addresses, e-surveys are being used more and more. But that is the problem. Whole demographic groups don't have e-mail addresses or do not use the Internet often enough to be willing participants. For those groups that do use it, however, it is wonderful.

Even current students can be a problem, depending on the campus system. In many instances, every student has an e-mail address assigned by the school. But they also have one they bring with them that they don't give up. In fact, they often use this other address more often. Therefore, don't assume that they see messages sent to their campus e-mail address.

For groups that are online often, e-mail surveys can be effective. Online response rates are high and very fast, and the cost is much less. You still need expert advice on questionnaire construction and results analysis, but the whole project is easier and more efficient.

One-on-One Interviews

Interviews can gather in-depth information and insight. In order to shape the right questions, they usually precede a survey or focus group. Or they may follow a survey or focus group to explore results and new ideas in greater depth, often with opinion leaders.

Interviews can be very helpful when used in the right way. They can be used with selective prospective students and parents to identify emerging trends and test new materials. They can be used with alumni leaders to evaluate programs and launch trial balloons. They can be used with donors to help shape case statements and evaluate potential giving levels. They can be used with media editors to explore interests and test ideas. They can be a rich source of new material.

Focus Groups

Focus groups of from six to 12 people elicit information about how well you are doing and what you should be doing. They can also be used to test new ideas or evaluate materials. They are usually led by trained facilitators and focus on a particular set of questions. Sometimes they are watched through a one-way mirror so body language can be observed, or electronic devices are used to register emotional and/or reasoned reactions to what subjects see or are told. Focus groups are almost always recorded so that a more careful content analysis can be made later.

Focus groups can be very helpful for marketing research, but they are more effective when used in conjunction with surveys and interviews. They can refine questions before surveys are conducted or explore implications after survey results are known. They can uncover ideas that can be explored in greater depth later with individuals in one-on-one interviews.

Hearing people responding to the facilitator's questions, then to each other's, then answering each other's objections and expanding on each other's ideas—all this can be very enlightening to the marketer. Along with providing information about how people think and feel, it provides depth of understanding and reveals new uses of language. The marketing communicator is always looking for new ways to say things, especially when describing the competitive advantage one more time. And focus groups often come forth with just the right words for this moment in time.

Many organizations do focus groups, but few do them well. Selecting participants is critical, and so is assessing the results. To present the different points of view of a variety of groups, some focus groups will have faculty, students, staff, alumni, and donors meeting together. But more often they will consist of homogenous groups—young alumni, second-semester freshman, etc. The results of the meetings are compared later. In all cases, careful preparation and analysis is essential for reaching reliable conclusions. It is safer to use objective external facilitators, even though all of us have people on board who feel competent to lead focus groups.

IMPORTANCE OF RESEARCH

Marketing research is essential. It should be ongoing. It therefore should receive a permanent line in the budget, if it doesn't already have one.

When properly designed, research focuses on specific market segments and asks only for information that is absolutely necessary for making decisions. Each project, therefore, can be modest in both size and cost. Getting started with an image survey is possible even for the smallest institution, even if it means not doing something else. It is imperative that you begin to base your decisions on this kind of information. Don't procrastinate doing the research.

Think of research as the feedback part of the whole communications process. When you think that way, there are many, many ways to gather information—methods beyond what I have described here. Use an evaluation card following every special event. Or enclose a response card with every magazine or with selected news releases. You might even employ admissions recruiters, alumni field officers, and fund raisers as information gatherers. Give them several questions to get answered as they visit people on their travels. Be sure the questions are worded so the results can be compiled and compared. Now you have a living research program with feedback arriving every day.

Don't let that long ago, huge, expensive survey that everyone hated frighten you. Show them how smaller, less expensive, more frequent projects can give you information you can use to make decisions and give everyone the confidence they need to break new ground.

CHAPTER EIGHT

On a Mission: Marketing Inside the Institution

Soon after launching an integrated marketing program, it becomes apparent that the internal community—faculty, students, and staff—constitutes a very important target market. The staff consists of exempt and nonexempt employees, both of which deserve equal attention.

Most institutions neglect internal communication and never consider internal marketing. Everyone knows internal communication is important, and everyone intends to do a better job. But when the goals are set and the tasks divided up among the communications staff, everyone needs to do the media relations, community relations, publications, magazine, special events, and other external projects as assigned. What gets done internally is a newsletter, and that's about it. Hardly anyone has ever even thought about internal marketing.

MISSION, VISION, AND VALUES

The topic comes up naturally during discussions about the challenge of getting everyone on the same page with respect to competitive advantage. If it is so important, how do we accomplish this? Indeed, the fact that internal communication quickly becomes external communication is very easy to understand. And to be sure, it would produce a major impact if everyone inside the institution had the same story to tell and took advantage of every opportunity to tell it. The objective is to mobilize the troops, and to do it will take a plan and a great deal of new activity.

Remember, the planning process really begins with clarifying mission, proceeds to stating the vision, and eventually completes the picture with a list of values. The central message that defines competitive advantage evolves from this. Eventually we want all students, faculty, and staff to know and to be able to articulate that central, identity-defining message. But what approach is likely to work? Will they buy a campaign to promote the message?

In some settings, a campaign to promote the institutional marketing message might work. But if the process of defining the mission was as participatory as it should have been, and if various segments of the institution were involved in reviewing it, then a follow-up program to get everyone familiar with it and able to recite it seems very likely to succeed. The best way to launch an internal marketing initiative is to build it around the mission statement—and let the rest of the message evolve over time from there.

LAUNCHING THE INITIATIVE

If possible, invite all faculty and staff to a luncheon to announce the initiative. Bring students into the project at an academic convocation or at any other event early in the year that student leaders attend. If the institution is too large for these activities, present the concept at a meeting or reception for opinion leaders of each group. Let all of these people see the mission statement on banners and plaques. Give everyone a coffee mug inscribed with the mission statement and ask them to put it on their desks. Give attendees a framed mission to hang on their office wall.

Ask the president to deliver remarks that remind everyone of how the mission statement came about, what it really means, and what is coming ahead with respect to the institution's plans to be more visible and more influential. Tell them how important it is to know the mission, comprehend the special competitive advantage, and tell the story at every opportunity.

FACULTY AND STAFF "ON-A-MISSION" RECOGNITION

Keep the campaign going by inviting everyone to nominate people whose work and life exemplify the institution's mission. Then honor these people at events and in publications. Write a brief statement describing the nominees, and publish their pictures in the campus internal newsletter. Recognize four or five at a time once or twice a month. Have the president send them a letter of congratulations or, better yet, deliver it to them in their office. This kind of recognition can go on for a long time, and each time the honor is made public it communicates loud and clear the mission statement and the need to tell the story far and wide.

Eventually this combination of events, presidential remarks, recognition programs, and publications can not only get everyone on the same page, it can reinforce all of the institution's traditions and strengthen its corporate culture. This will foster a stronger sense of team and ownership for the goal of greater distinction and more visibility. Everyone will begin to do his or her part, instead of just expecting someone else to do it. This is what makes it marketing instead of just internal communication.

You can also offer to bring more information about the message and marketing activities to faculty meetings, staff meetings, and other internal events. You can report on the marketing-task-force activities, ask for reaction to new ideas, let people critique new publications, and ask for overall impressions of how things are going. The whole idea is to get people involved, listen to what they say, and do what you can.

NEW EMPLOYEE AND STAFF ORIENTATION

Most new-employee orientation programs cover institutional history, how the place is organized, traditions, and benefits. What is not is explained is why the place is so special and that all employees are responsible for communicating this to everyone they come into contact with. The orientation session is a great time to do this because new employees are excited about their new jobs and anxious to feel that the organization is special. They are receptive to the message and actually appreciate it.

Give them a soft briefcase and/or a shirt bearing the institutional logo. Give them a coffee mug or a bookmark inscribed with the mission statement. Give them a four-color brochure that tells your story dramatically and concisely. Emphasize the importance of teamwork and how this institution is a strong family-like community. Make it a powerful moment when you welcome them to the next chapter in their life's adventure. Take advantage of this once-in-an-employment opportunity to motivate a feeling of pride in their choice.

INTERNAL PUBLICATIONS

Internal publications need to reflect the overall marketing orientation of the institution. While reporting about events and activities, they need to reinforce the central message, repeat the mission in various ways, have the appropriate institutional "look," and be sensitive to building community and reinforcing the right cultural values. When these messages are consistently present and stories are selected that reinforce them, internal communications will move the place forward.

Perform a communications audit of internal publications to determine the presence of the competitive advantage message and appropriate design. Internal publications should cover news and activities objectively and clearly. They should not become overt marketing pieces, but they should portray the marketing initiative as big news and see the stories that reinforce the major message points as the major stories. This editorial framework also accommodates hard news and the controversial issues of the day. Telling and reinforcing the institutional story in no way prevents you from telling the bad news as well.

CLIENT/STUDENT SERVICE TRAINING

Customer service is a hot topic in business. A satisfied customer means both repeat and new business. In education, a satisfied student becomes an adult-education student and brings new business as well. Research indicates that a good percentage of new students attend schools because they know someone who is or was there. This kind of business costs much less to develop, and it can, through families, become self-perpetuating.

It is self-defeating to treat students like children who do not need to be served, or that because we are not a business we don't have to believe the customer is always right. Besides, work is less fun when you approach it with a negative attitude, and one person in an office who feels this way can sour the whole climate. A positive tone, willingness to help, and a controlled temper is the key to relationship building. It begins with the campus police officer who helps a visitor find a parking space instead of writing a ticket.

Accomplishing this with all frontline staff usually requires training. Even though we are in the education business, we have traditionally done very little management and customer-service training. Most canned programs don't work in our setting, and a lot of customer-service subject matter seems too commercial and trivial. What is better is a series of quality meetings where employees share the problems they face and then brainstorm positive ways to deal with them. In the context of these meetings, employees get ideas about how important all of this is to the future of the institution and the future livelihood of everyone in the meeting. Employees end up liking these kinds of meetings. Like discussions of mission, vision, and values, these problem-solving conversations are bonding experiences for the participants.

MANAGEMENT COMMUNICATION

People want their bosses to give them information about work issues and announcements. If they don't get it from the source they expect, they will deny knowing it, even if they get it from some other source. Communication within the management structure is critical, and no company publication can compensate for its absence. Organizational unit heads must assume their communication responsibilities or employees will complain that "they never tell us anything." This needs to begin with top management. If teamwork and participatory processes are important—and they are essential if integrated marketing is to be practiced—then the president needs to model this more open style of planning and managing.

One way to do this is with an integrated marketing task force because it includes the best talent from all over campus. As discussed previously, this gets people out of normal channels and opens communication in a healthy way. The problems it creates are minor, and the advantages it produces are long lasting—better ideas more forcefully implemented by highly motivated and talented people.

Another very compatible way is for the president to ask most everyone who reports to a vice president to meet periodically with him or her and the vice presidents to discuss annual goals, important accomplishments, and any other concerns. These meetings can be a combination of off-site retreats and shorter on-campus breakfasts or luncheons. At first they are deeply appreciated but a bit restrained. But in time the group gets comfortable and begins to discuss institutional issues, including the work of the marketing task force. Relationships strengthen, mutual respect develops, and everyone learns that no one's authority is compromised. Daily business still works fine within organizational structures, and everyone feels better informed, more highly motivated, and intensely committed to making the whole place better.

E-mail is a wonderful support tool for this kind of management team building. You can set up a modified listserv where team members can communicate with each other on issues and ideas. Any member who has an idea or wants to test a presentation on the group can put it online for comment and discussion. The group might even adopt a name. One team took the name of the retreat site where it had its first meeting. From that time on, team members referred to the group and its ongoing organizational development agenda with a kind of pride.

The president can also use e-mail to keep the group intact and in touch. He or she can send periodic FYI bulletins or drafts of goals for early comment, ask for input on issues and problems, and keep them informed on financial developments. And occasionally the president can send update-type state-of-the-institution reports to the entire university community, including trustees. This combination of group meetings and e-mail creates an extremely strong relationship-building strategy, much stronger than either one alone.

COMMUNICATION WITH STUDENTS

Communication with students is usually more difficult than it should be. There are so many of them that no efficient method or channel exists. That may be changing with the Internet.

The equivalent of the house organ doesn't usually exist for students. And the student newspaper is usually too independent to provide the necessary kind of marketing information. This leaves direct mail (which usually winds up on the floor outside mailboxes), personal calls to residence halls and clubs, message and bulletin boards in student centers, and the Internet.

Direct mail can work for invitations to meetings where messages are presented. Message boards can display mission statements. Personal appearances at residence-hall meetings and clubs can be very effective but time consuming. You can achieve the same impact with students that you do by meeting with faculty and staff.

The problem is finding the people and time to conduct this kind of communication. One answer is to recruit talented students, train them, and then pay them a small stipend to tell the story to student groups. They can find very creative ways to present the mission, get students to discuss it, and get them to see how important all of this is to the reputation of the place they will soon graduate from. You won't get everyone, but you never do. Some faculty and staff hold out too. But many students do respond well, and the ones who do form a powerful network of word-of-mouth champions. Your student communicators might be so effective that you use them to visit staff and faculty meetings as well, solving still another time-management problem.

Communication with students should also center on the Internet; in some cases, closed-circuit cable TV might be used. Of course the effectiveness of the cable-TV channel depends on its utilization. Kiosks and posters can communicate mission statements and themes. The Internet is no doubt the better choice to build relationships, but this again will depend on whether or not a majority of students use their campus e-mail accounts or another one, as many do. If they can be reached, online e-surveys generate the interaction and the feeling of being heard. Even in the age of digital communication, however, the kind of relationship building required for marketing is better in person.

What turns internal communication into marketing is the participatory process you establish. To internal publications and periodicals, we add on-a-mission campaigns, recognition programs, new-employee orientation modules, better-edited publications, client/student service training, innovative management-communication meetings, and better ways of involving students. In the final analysis, powerful internal communication can become your most effective and far-reaching external communication, and if you can get a good portion of the troops onboard, you will have a real marketing machine.

CHAPTER NINE

Getting More Visibility: The Impact of Marketing on the Office of Communication

"We cannot take on another project until we stop doing something." That is what most office of communication professionals feel every day of their life. There are calendars to update, press releases to write, phone calls to return, mail and e-mail to answer. People ask for help with brochures and flyers, civic clubs call for help finding speakers, reporters need an expert on this or that, colleagues drop in to talk, and there just isn't enough time in the day. There is no time to be proactive, but marketing requires the communication office to be proactive.

Marketing sets priorities and asks that reputation-defining themes be repeated over and over. It also asks that stories and illustrations be found to support and advance them. It requires communications to be edited and orchestrated to clarify competitive advantage and make certain the world knows about the institution's strengths. It insists that issues be identified and crises be anticipated so that problems can be managed effectively and in line with the institution's values and culture.

How can you decide what *not* to do so that you can become more proactive? Most offices find it next to impossible to make that decision. Everything seems to be vital and important. The only approach that seems to work is to change the way you decide what to do each day.

Begin with the mission statement. Put it on the wall. Then clarify the message themes that the institution will use to state its competitive advantage. If there is a marketing task force at work, it should produce it. Put it on the wall. Get a copy of the university goals and put them on the wall as well. Now write a mission statement for the communications operation and a set of goals that advance the institution's goals. With all of this at hand, decide who will do what to meet these goals, planning a calendar of activities for several weeks at a time.

The challenge now is to stay focused on the goals and their related tasks. Certainly, urgent surprises will often come, but unless they are of crisis magnitude, stick to the plan. When someone drops in with an urgent but unimportant press release to write, simply refer to your work schedule and say the request needs to be made in advance and go through an editorial process. Explain that press releases are written only when they advance a goal.

Now you say, "That will never work in my institution. They will eat me alive!" But they will eat you alive only if you don't take the time to visit each academic dean and key department head to explain this policy. Tell them that you are now working from a plan to advance the institution and that the plan has specific goals. Explain that many of the press releases you write are a waste of time because you know in advance they won't get published. Ask them to understand that you can no longer take the time to go through that exercise. But suggest that you can sit down and help them design a comprehensive communication plan for their area so all can see what actual news stories they have to tell and what other more effective communications initiatives they can take.

UNDERSTANDING THE NEWS BUSINESS

Many believe that it is the responsibility of the news business to promote community organizations, that newspapers and broadcasters are public services and that helping you achieve *your* goals is one of *their* goals. Not really. They are interested in promoting their organization and their own profits, not yours. News is a business.

The news business, for the most part, does what we advocate doing for education. They clarify what business they are in and then set goals based on meeting the needs of their primary market segments. Because they are a mass media, they serve large numbers people—far more than your stakeholders and opinion leaders—and they perform research to determine what those large numbers want to receive.

For example, you may be a small private school, and you may be the only university in your city. Your constituents may not understand why your local newspaper gives the larger public university in another part of the state greater coverage than it gives yours. They don't understand that thousands more graduates of that public university live in your city than people associated with your institution. The news business plays to subscribers, and you have to understand their market in order to understand their choices. In the final analysis, they are not in the business of promoting your institution. They leave that to you.

They will report the news, however, and so successful media relations are a matter of matching their goals and yours. When you make that match, you have the potential for big coverage. The trick is to do more by doing less. Find those stories and put more effort into getting all the information together and marketing the story to the news media.

Of course, since the news media will also report the bad news, it is critical to be prepared. In the course of pitching stories, you need to build relationships that will be useful in times of crisis. Being prepared and willing to deal with sensitive issues is an important part of the work. More about that later.

TAKING AN INTERNAL AGENCY APPROACH

To implement your goals, you will require a comprehensive communication plan. Your plan will have a media-relations component, but it will also require other initiatives such as advertising, special events, personal visits, invitations, communications with opinion leaders and stakeholders, and more. The communication staff will now be thinking about integrated communications and developing tactics for getting all of these things done. They will be thinking more strategically about how to achieve goals and advance the institution.

The principle that should guide the selection of stories to pitch to the news media is *reputation defining.*

With this comprehensive plan in hand, the next task is to sit down with each dean and major unit head and suggest that a plan that ties their areas to the overall plan. These area plans will have the same kind of components—some media relations objectives but other objectives as well. Now you decide who does what, with some of the tasks performed by the central communication office and others handled by the unit itself. With the plan, everyone is pulling in the same direction.

Keep in mind that by "plan" we really mean an outline or blueprint. List the goals and identify what needs to be done to meet them. Then develop a separate schedule of who actually does what by when. Keep it close at hand so that it can be reworked as circumstances change. Do not write comprehensive detailed documents; their contents will not be remembered and they will not get implemented.

What you are really doing is internal strategic-communication counseling. After the plan is developed and central messages understood, you will be in a position to advise all institutional executives on speeches and public statements, the handling of sensitive issues, etc., all the while reminding everybody that their ultimate challenge is to uphold the values and reinforce the competitive advantage.

REPUTATION-DEFINING STORIES

The principle that should guide the selection of stories to pitch to the news media is *reputation defining*. The more you talk about this, the more sense it will make. The more people understand it, the less they will expect you to place weak stories. Once they see how a comprehensive plan works much better, deans and department heads will help you explain it to faculty and staff. One way to get a dean's or vice president's help is to say, "Please help me avoid writing non-news news releases. But when you have a situation that for political reasons you want me to try, just call and let me know." That makes them feel important, and you will find they do help you and rarely call.

A reputation-defining story is one that reinforces one of your priority centers of excellence. These naturally get identified as a part of the planning process. The marketing task force will discuss and identify them. They will also be discussed in cabinet and other management meetings, and they will be discussed and identified in the comprehensive and area communication plans. Any disagreements must be reconciled, but you may be surprised to see more agreement than you thought you would.

It is important to identify these centers of excellence in the communication plan, but they do not have to be labeled as such in public. In reality, all academic programs need to be communicated as high quality—but some will be lifted a bit higher than others as reputation-building opportunities. Over time, this list might vary as needs and situations change. Academic programs rise and fall in quality over time, and market conditions change, making some programs more interesting in the marketplace at one time than at another. Engineering is hot, then it isn't. Nursing schools attract students, then fade. Reputation is built on a combination of true academic quality and the ability to connect programs of current interest to market needs.

QUOTING EXPERTS

In addition to reputation-defining stories, you also need to search for quotable experts. These are usually faculty members who can respond to reporters' questions when their subject is in the news. These people should be identified in advance, listed in an expert's guide that is circulated to the news media, and given some training about what to expect and how to handle media questions. This is a very important way of giving the institution more visibility in the news media, and you should spend more time doing it well than on sending out press releases.

You need to decide whether or not it is cost-beneficial to employ a national media consultant. Some of your reputation-defining stories may make it to the national press, but many of those will only run once. Your experts are more likely to get quoted in national trend stories where they may be used repeatedly. Even so, only a small portion of your target market will see these stories and quotes as they appear. You can, however, send these clips directly to your constituents to reinforce your image as a nationally significant institution.

VISIBILITY WITH WHOM AT WHAT COST?

When your constituents tell you the institution is not visible enough, they seem to expect to see your name written across the sky. Most communications professionals, no matter the institution they serve, have heard the complaint, "We are tired of being the best-kept secret. Why doesn't the news media ever report about us?" Somehow your supporters always see the one time the newspaper covers your competitor but misses the 10 stories about you. You would think it would be the opposite, that their love of the institution would make them psychologically inclined to notice everything you do. Not so. They see and resent what the other guy does and think no one in your place is doing the job. It is the same for every institution, even many on the top tier. What is the strategic solution to this dilemma?

What these complainers are really saying is that *they* are missing what you are doing. They are not in the right place at the right time to get the full message. The strategic solution is to send the message directly to them. If you can get all of the people in each target market that control the future and health of your institution to *think* you are visible, then for all practical purposes you are. The strategic solution is to build your communications around direct and interactive media wherever and whenever possible.

STAKEHOLDERS AND OPINION LEADERS

It is difficult to find the time to build mailing and e-mail lists for all stakeholders in all target market segments. But it is well worth the time. The more you get into marketing, the more you will see the value of the relationships you build by communicating directly with these key people.

Remember the two-step flow theory of communication? You communicate with the opinion leaders and they influence the others. It really works. It takes some time, but it gains momentum the more you do it.

Set up an address system that includes opinion leaders inside and outside the institution. Separate those with active e-mail addresses from those who must be reached by regular mail. Include phone numbers in the system. Send an initial mailing telling them that as an insider you are putting them on a prestige list to receive special insider reports and information. Include a return card asking first if they want to stay on this list and then for the "best" postal address, e-mail address, and phone number.

Set up a system where they receive something at least monthly. Send them news clips several times a year to demonstrate how often you appear in the news media. Send them a copy of important stories. When warranted, send them the news release. You might want to send them a version of the university goals and reports that the president usually sends only to trustees. Send them special announcements of events. Send them invitations to plays, art openings, and special athletics tournaments and events. Offer them tickets to sit in special sections. Ask for their feedback with each mailing. And—this is important—ask them to provide word-of-mouth support. Remind them of your central niche-defining message, and ask them to repeat it everywhere they go. But always make them feel important and address them as VIPs.

Over time, large numbers of people will feel, individually, that you treat them well. They will feel like insiders and gradually forge a bond that will become your real competitive advantage. These people will feel more comfortable relating to your institution. They will feel familiar with you and your people, and they will prefer to do their education business with you.

LEVERAGING PARTNERSHIPS

Associating with the right people and organizations produces instant visibility. Picking those partnerships is critical, but developing the right ones can not only broaden your programming and influence, it can lift your profile at very low cost.

One private institution, looking for a way to promote its new program in international diplomacy, realized the potential of having the right international partner. By forming a partnership with the United Nations Association, it instantly established an international presence. At no cost, its new partner used its communication channels and resources to tell the world about the new program.

It is also important to remember that newspapers and broadcasters have advertising and promotion departments. While the news department might not view a particular event as news, the advertising department might be eager to co-sponsor it. When this kind of deal is made, the newspaper or broadcast station will usually use its own advertising space to promote the event at low or no charge to you. You provide the management and venue, and they provide the promotion. A great partnership!

TCU put together a leadership program involving top students at schools throughout Latin America. They asked American Airlines to sponsor the program. Now the airline can brag that it helped develop the next generation of leaders for all of Latin America, and TCU gets some cash, airline tickets, and instant visibility in a market that is important to its international studies goals.

Finding strategic partnerships is the way to develop a lot of new educational opportunities. This is true for business and communication internships, continuing- education programs, technical research, fine-arts programs, healthcare projects, and more. It is also true for gaining visibility and building prestige. You are whom you associate with. But remember this has a down side when your partner is an organization of lesser stature or the agreement goes sour. Make sure it is a clear gain for your institution before you launch the deal.

STRATEGIC SPECIAL EVENTS

Special events take on new importance in an integrated marketing program. As that importance is recognized, the office of communication becomes more and more involved. Unless one is already on board, a case is made for hiring a special-events specialist who would become a part of all strategy sessions and goal setting.

Live events satisfy all of the requirements for relationship building. They target market segments, provide direct communication with constituents, feature immediate feedback and interactive opportunities, and provide ample opportunity to reinforce central niche-defining messages. You can transmit simple information and control the total environment and setting. You have the unique opportunity to communicate multi-sensory messages: posters, banners, displays, slide shows, videos, audio, etc. The impact can be strongly emotional and yet leave the attendee with a message. And it is possible to evaluate results quickly and meaningfully. Events are also opportunities for partnerships.

The lesson here is to never miss an opportunity with a special event. Never think of events as just receptions or just parties. Think of them as interactive relationship-building opportunities. Make certain to put messages in the environment and seek feedback. Think of anniversaries as a time to revisit the founding mission and current vision. See inaugurations as launching a new day with new goals. See fund-raising kickoff celebrations as occasions for emotional bonding. Never miss an opportunity to recognize achievement or service. Commencements are times to remind everyone of family and institutional ties. Groundbreakings and dedications are opportunities to inspire performance in specific areas and programs. Focus more on the communication that is taking place, and take every opportunity to make it happen. The more you think about it, the more important special events will become.

DIRECT AND INTERACTIVE MEDIA

The biggest change in the office of communication is that, in this age of new technology, direct and interactive communication has become more effective than the mass media. As the meaning and implications of this sinks in, what people do with their time undergoes dramatic change. Now communicators focus on target markets or audiences and look for ways to get the message directly to them. They are aware of the central niche-defining messages and select other stories and events to reinforce them.

What is most surprising is that while fewer press releases are sent, more events receive coverage. This can happen because, by understanding the goals of the news business, you have found stories that are more likely to be used. And by better understanding your goals, you have come to realize that if your stakeholders and opinion leaders are connected, you are doing your job.

Also, as an integrated program develops, the office of communication becomes more involved with advertising initiatives, branding activities, and management of issues and crises. To be effective, advertising must connect to all of the institution's communication initiatives. The perception of your brand is the sum total of all communications, and the way you manage issues and crises has enormous marketing consequences. All of this is addressed in the pages ahead.

CHAPTER TEN

Integrated Marketing and Managing Issues

Issues and crisis management is usually considered a pure public relations function. But when performing the analysis associated with planning integrated marketing, it soon becomes clear just how important to the effectiveness of the overall program it is to handle issues well. There are issues of opportunity and issues of vulnerability—and you need to have strategies for both. Your marketing blueprint should indicate which issues are going to be used to generate visibility and the perception of social and industry leadership, and it should identify the issues that you are monitoring because they have the capacity to damage the overall marketing program.

OPPORTUNITIES AND VULNERABILITIES

First of all, dealing with issues is a very important part of any media relations program. You might be proactive on some issues and at other times get out in front quickly when a negative situation appears. Either way, working with the news media on all facets of issues is a large part of building relationships with them.

Also, how the institution handles issues will form the public impression of it. Issues management is a major factor of your image. An issue handled well creates a positive impression even when the situation is negative. An issue handled badly produces a bad impression every time. It is worth the time to take issues management very seriously.

Some issues actually provide special opportunities for institutions. Because of a match between its interests and a public need, a particular issue becomes a leadership opportunity, an opportunity to step out with a solution or point of view that gains the institution both visibility and respect. When it comes to marketing, it is very important to take issues into account in the planning process.

For example, the public impression that higher education is overpriced may be a reason to proactively address that issue in the marketing program. Or the fact that safety is a concern to parents may be a reason to deal with that issue up front with comparative statistics and a well-defined campus initiative that becomes a marketing theme. Issues that can make an institution look current and socially relevant can be used effectively in presidential speeches, as news stories, in newsletters, or even in marketing materials. Develop an institutional position paper, and then use its substance in a variety of presentations and materials.

Of course, every institution has many vulnerabilities. There are issues everywhere that can instantly become negative news stories. Charges of financial mismanagement, crimes on campus, student behavior problems, chemicals in laboratories, a tornado, a terrorist act, a residence hall fire—all of these and many more can be instant nightmares for communicators. The more they are anticipated and the more staff plans processes for handling them, the more the marketing program stays on track.

THE ISSUES MANAGEMENT PROCESS

There are six steps in the issues management process, and an integrated marketing task force and the office of communication should review them once or twice a year.

1. *Identification.* Scan publications and news media to determine what issues are getting public attention. Develop the habit of doing this as you go about your work. Also assign this to a student assistant. This is a very good project for interns.

2. *Selection.* Sort the issues that relate to your industry and institution into two lists: opportunities and vulnerabilities. Interns can do this in conjunction with staff, or this can be a great exercise for a retreat. The exercise can include identifying what research needs to be done and how the issue might be managed.
3. *Research.* Investigate and gather data on the issue. An intern under professional staff supervision can do this, but, if it is an issue of major opportunity or major concern, a professional staff member should do the work. Develop a file for each issue and assemble a "library" of material. The research also should produce a fact sheet or a position paper or both.
4. *Communication.* Develop a strategic communications plan for each major issue just as if it were an academic program or center of excellence. The plan will take into account implications on media relations but focus on target market segments and favor direct and interactive media. As with your other activities, focus on stakeholders and opinion leaders.
5. *Evaluation.* Evaluation is difficult to quantify, but you can get a good idea how you are doing by seeking feedback each time you communicate. A lot of people will let you know how they feel about issues, but usually these people are at both extremes. Either they like what you are doing or they don't. Feedback is necessary to get an accurate idea of what most people think and how they feel.
6. *Thinking strategy.* Remind yourself about the different opinions that appear inside each market segment. Some will already agree with your position, some will oppose it, and some will have no opinion. Reinforce the ones who are with you. Don't worry about the ones who are against you—they will be very hard to convert. Focus on those without opinions because, combined with those who already support you, they should produce a nice majority in your favor. If you can't make this formula work, you should probably avoid the issue.

CRISIS COMMUNICATION

Crises always occur at the most inconvenient time. It is late at night and you have had several glasses of wine when the call comes. You hope it will go away. There is no way you want to deal with this now. But this clearly is not the time to go to bed and hope for the best. Somehow you have to remember how important it is to take action and to do it with confidence.

Handling crises well is critical to an institution's image and identity. More than anything else, a crisis situation will either reinforce your institutional values or undermine their credibility. Public opinion can change in an instant, and a reputation that took years to build can shatter literally overnight.

Crisis Policies

Policies are principles that guide the development of practice. Since no two crises are exactly alike, it is helpful to adopt policies to guide your response.

1. *Determine who will be responsible for managing communication during a crisis.* Usually this is the communication director.
2. *Outline procedures for gathering facts.* Unless you know exactly what happened based on your own investigation, you will have to accept as fact what the news media give you.
3. *Define what you believe to be "in the public's interest" to know and what you consider to be private matters.* This is important because it is where you may have differences with reporters, and you need to be clear in your own mind what legitimately should remain private.
4. *Assign someone to develop a basic fact sheet and write statements for your spokespeople.* Choose a public spokesperson. Only the CEO? Only the communication director? Or will you use several spokespeople determined by their areas of responsibility and how well they can perform on their feet? In all cases, the director of communication will have to coach spokespeople to keep them on-message and to avoid being put on the defensive by reporters.

Procedures for Handling a Crisis

Go over the steps for handling a crisis with your staff several times a year. It may be difficult to find the time, but once a crisis strikes nothing else matters. There is no other news.

1. *Develop a fact sheet.* Include everything except material you deem to be private, i.e., student records, personnel records, highly personal information about individuals, etc.
2. *Form a crisis communication committee.* Include the director of communication, director of media relations, internal communications director, an expert from the unit closest to the crisis, possibly the campus security chief, etc.
3. *Identify priority audiences.* Begin with victims, then internal people, then the news media, and, beyond that, the stakeholders and opinion leaders in each of your priority market segments.
4. *Make a plan of action.* It should answer the question, "What are you doing about this?"
5. *Use the fact sheets to prepare statements for each spokesperson.*
6. *Rehearse the spokespeople.* Brainstorm anticipated questions and ways to answer them.
7. *Choose a method of release.* Press conference? E-mail? Regular press release?
8. *Determine how calls will be handled following the press conference or release.*
9. *Develop an issues-management program to help prevent crises.* Prevention is the best strategy—and some crises are preventable. But in today's changing and competitive world, most significant organizations cannot avoid crises. When you are a player in the community and are serving all kinds of people, crises become regular facts of life. This is why anticipating all developments, positive and negative, and anticipating crises whenever you can becomes a practical aspect of developing marketing and communication plans.

GOVERNMENT RELATIONS

Some people think "issues management" means "government relations" because the techniques of issues management were initially devised to identify and track public issues for the purpose of lobbying. Today, the techniques are helpful for managing all issues. We should, however, consider the value of government relationships as a part of overall marketing. Along with helping you influence legislation critical to education, they help you with student recruiting, fund raising, and, therefore, overall reputation building and visibility. Being perceived as a power in the city, state, or nation is a reputation-building factor to be sure.

Governments are separate market segments in your marketing blueprint, and are more or less important depending on your location and ambitions. Put them in your planning not just for legislative matters, but for their overall role in enhancing your image as forward-looking.

CHAPTER ELEVEN

Building Reputation: The Power of Branding

The concept of "the brand" comes up during every discussion of institutional marketing. We know that visibility within target markets is essential. And most of us believe, based on research performed by ourselves or others, that name recognition strongly influences perceptions of quality. In fact, many believe in the "Chivas Regal effect," which suggests that the better known your name, the higher you can set your price. The concept of brand relates to all of this.

WHAT IS A BRAND?

I have defined the terms *market position*, *niche*, and *competitive advantage*:

- *Market position* is how consumers differentiate you from your competitors, the special slot in their mind that you occupy.
- *Niche*, a different way of saying the same thing, is the special place in the market that differentiates you.
- *Competitive advantage* is still another way of saying the same thing except that it presents this difference in comparison to your competitors—better in overall quality or better in that you offer a unique service or have a unique way of delivering it.

All of these terms are different ways of seeing or describing your unique identity.

Branding is still another way to think about identity. A brand is what your customer feels when he or she sees or thinks of your name. It's the sum total of that person's experiences of your institution. It's an emotion. It is a feeling that has meaning to the consumer because it credibly ties the institution to what makes the consumer feel good. The consumer has a feeling that translates as compatibility: I can associate with this place because I feel better when I am connected to this feeling.

A brand-produced feeling leads to a perception of a special kind of quality of product or service. It is a technical place or a friendly place or a challenging place or an openly spiritual place. Or it stands for a particular approach to religion, or it is an arty place, or it is a studious place: Any one of many possible feelings could become associated with a name. The name may also suggest a particular set of values or a culture. It might stand for rugged individualism or individual freedom or community or social service. Or it might be a place with strong traditions, such as uniforms, special ceremonies, and disciplined behaviors. Any of these feelings, when connected to a name, can turn that name into a brand.

A brand must be relevant to perceived needs. The consumer must make that connection. The name therefore gives the consumer a feeling of confidence. Because the place knows who it is and what it is doing, it must communicate boldly and clearly so that it *really* looks like it knows what it's doing. A brand is a connection, a bonding, a relationship. When the consumer thinks of it, he or she feels comfortable with what the name stands for and confident that it will deliver.

Therefore, a brand is also a promise. It promises consumers that all of their anticipated feelings will always be reinforced by contact with the actual products or services. That means the institution must deliver, because one significant disappointment can quickly change brand perception. Promises must be kept in the world of brands. One bad meal in a great brand-name restaurant, and the customer is likely to never go back.

Brands are ultimately shaped more by what you do than by what you say. This is why it is so important to understand the difference between marketing and marketing communication. As we have said, marketing considers product, price, distribution, and communication together at the same time. And, once again, this is essential to ascertaining that your products and distribution deliver the promises made in your communications. Brand development is much more than communication.

BRAND EQUITY

Brand equity is the notion that your brand has a tangible value. Your brand is an organizational asset. The perception of the sum total of what makes your institution significant and the feelings associated with it is what establishes your institution's net worth in the marketplace. Any investment made to develop the brand is an actual, tangible investment in the development of the institution. If you ever try to sell it, the value of your name brand would establish your price.

THE WAY BRANDS WORK

Your brand is name awareness plus identifying defining impressions. It exists in the minds of consumers. But if your name is not in the minds of consumers, the task of building a relationship is that much more difficult. Imagine calling on a high school counselor who never heard of your school. The communication task is far different from calling on a counselor who not only knows your name but has a positive impression of what that name means in terms of service quality and style. The real value of brand is the way a powerful one can produce a climate of receptivity before you try to make the sale. Your brand exists out there in the universe, transcending the actual products or service. Its independent presence and perceived value are relatively permanent, so long as actual experience of it does not disappoint.

THE IMPORTANCE OF GRAPHIC IDENTITY

Graphic identity is critical to the development and maintenance of brand name. People in an institution will come to appreciate why consistent use of the logo, design standards, and colors are so important to the success of a marketing program.

Effective marketing communications feature consistent themes and facts that stand for an institution's mission, vision, and values. Over time, these themes and facts become niche-defining thoughts and feelings. Eventually these thoughts and feelings become associated with the name, logo, distinctive colors, and design elements that appear with them. When the institution's name and/or logo evokes unique niche-defining and character-defining thoughts and feelings, the institution has become a "brand."

WHAT'S IN A NAME?

Name is important in branding. It should be relatively short. It should have an easy memory quality. And it should have intrinsic value to constituents who see or hear it.

Some university names are too long. In these cases, many end up using acronyms. This is not a perfect tradeoff because the complete name still has to be used from time to time, and the letters may carry little emotional and graphic potential. Since changing the name of an institution is far more difficult and expensive than making the letters work, you must make the most of what you have. Take care in how you present the name, how it looks on the page, and what you do with design and accompanying words to enhance any compelling meaning it might have.

GIVING SHAPE TO THE BRAND

The words used to describe the institution—what I previously referred to as the "central identity-defining message" or the "competitive advantage-defining message"—also helps define the brand. When choosing the words, take into account the strong emotional element in the way the consumer fits the perception into the brain. The words should have a self-fulfilling quality about them, promise individual gratification, but also remain credible. They should above all differentiate your institution.

TAG LINES

No tag line is better than a bad tag line. A bad tag line is one that adds nothing of value to the perception of the name. A bad tag line is one that conveys a message or feeling that conflicts with the identity-defining central messages that describe the institution. A bad tag line is one that is overused or sounds like a cliché.

A good tag line sums up in a few words what the central messages really mean. A good tag line is unique to you but has a familiar ring. A good tag line looks good in print with your logo. A good tag line is easily remembered. A good tag line is worth a thousand words. But it must be a good one.

A really good tag line goes a long way toward shaping and later sustaining the feelings evoked by the name. The sustaining part is very important because the ultimate objective is to have the brand established so powerfully that when the name is seen— sometimes in conjunction with the tag line and sometimes alone—it conveys all the feelings and emotions of all of the messages. That tag line fills out the name and adds substance to it when it's seen.

Good tag lines can be hard to come by. A marketing task force or communications staff can brainstorm hours and only get frustrated. They end up listing a hundred or more phrases only to conclude they have not yet found it. It's best not to use any tag line than to go with a weak one. Make the tag line brainstorming session a regular feature of periodic retreats, and use one when you come up with a good one. But don't add one until you're sure of it, and you think you can use it for a long time.

SUB-BRANDS

Schools, colleges, academic departments, and other programs within the organization sometimes need a distinctive identity within the overall institutional identity or brand. This occurs when the internal unit is communicating with a specific market segment that has specific and unique expectations, such as athletics fans, fine-arts supporters, or MBA prospects. In these cases, sub-brands are established that appeal to these markets but retain the look and feel of the overall institutional family.

A graphics standards manual is critical to integrated marketing success, but it cannot be too inflexible. Instead of beginning with the stance that university units must conform to central standards, begin by acknowledging that many units have legitimate claims to be sub-brands and that you are willing to work with them to assess their needs and define their sub-brand.

Assessment involves determining whether or not a department's claim for sub-brand status is legitimate based on an analysis of its marketplace. If the claim cannot be sustained, deny the request—but at least a lot of communication has taken place about how these decisions are made. Many academic departments cannot sustain this claim, but several may have a legitimate claim and in these cases you are in a position to shape the identity so that it reinforces the overall institutional look and message. In reality, most departments will make no claim at all.

A standards manual will show the official logo and accepted modifications. It will show the mascot and accepted modifications. It will show the tag line and how it should look on a page. It will give the PMS numbers for official colors. It will indicate acceptable uses of all this for publications, advertising, stationery, business cards, Web pages, and university vehicles. It will provide standards that achieve a look, but it will not eliminate creativity or end up being too inflexible. In the final analysis, you want cooperation and you don't want to have to be the logo police department. That is not what the marketing program needs.

THE ROLE OF ADVERTISING

The conventional wisdom for many in higher education used to be that advertising was too expensive, and that if you had to use it you were probably in trouble. Those who advertised were seen as desperate. But when integrated thinking became a part of strategic thinking, advertising started to look a bit different.

First, just as with research, thinking in terms of specific market segments changes where you consider buying advertising, and both the media and the limited focus make the situation more affordable. Even so, since saturation is important in advertising, you need to make a certain amount of commitment.

Second, when you think about integrated communication, you are thinking about all of the tools in the communication toolbox and how they work together. You don't expect an advertisement to work alone; rather it plays a role in a mix of communication. Considered this way, an advertisement may seem very important.

Third, when you think about branding, the special emotional power of advertising, combined with all of your other communications, becomes very compelling. Advertising allows you to shape your brand identity with a great deal of professional precision by combining powerful images with carefully crafted words. Repeated over and over, your advertisements serve as a foundation influence for shaping your other communications and activities.

In integrated marketing, advertising is used in two ways: to establish presence and as a part of a larger communication campaign. For example, one small college was located in a part of the city where it remained largely invisible. It was very difficult for the school to be perceived as a player in the community. A trustee decided to finance a billboard on the freeway that everyone driving into the city would see. From that moment on, no one in the city could overlook that institution. That billboard established a presence downtown for that college. It was now a larger part of that community.

Advertising is also used as a part of a larger campaign. One university advertises in a statewide magazine to establish a niche in the minds of state leaders, as well as in the minds of parents of prospective students. This is a high-circulation magazine to which many leaders subscribe that has a long shelf life on coffee tables and in waiting rooms. The strategy is to communicate an impressive message that has a "Wow, look at what they are doing" impact on the parents at the time when direct mail to prospective students is arriving in their homes. Timing the advertisements with the mailings makes the total package work.

GOOD NEWS AND BAD

The stronger and more established your brand name, the more effective your overall marketing program. The greater power your name has in the marketplace, the more important you become. Marketing becomes easier as your brand becomes more influential.

Young people respond well to brands, and they are always looking for new ones. A brand of shoe or clothes or school can become hot very quickly and everyone one wants one. Once the buzz is on the Internet, a phenomenon that professionals are learning to produce, you can become *the* place to be. That's the good news.

The bad news is that, with young people, brand trends can change very quickly. Becoming and remaining a brand of choice will be a real challenge in the 21st century. But with well-defined target markets, ongoing research into what people are thinking and feeling, and an integrated approach to brand development, you have the tools to stay on top of this rapidly changing world.

MIXING MEDIA FOR BRANDING

Since your objective is to be the brand of choice within specific target markets, you must choose a mix of media that works in each target and a mix that you can afford. Your advertising choices will include

- Targeted magazines, journals, and periodicals
- Events, sports printed programs
- News, "leadership" circulation magazines
- Newspapers
- Radio
- TV, cable TV
- Movie theaters
- Web ads
- Billboards
- Bus cards, bus bench cards
- Internal corporate publications

Magazine and periodical advertising really requires saturation to establish a presence with the readership. Unless you can buy several insertions, it's probably a waste of money. Events printed program advertising is a good way to establish presence and an implied partnership. Advertising in arts programs, for example, can be very effective branding for some institutions.

Newspaper advertising is most effective for specific program and events promotion. Although institutional advertising in special education sections is rarely effective, institutions sometimes feel they must do it for political reasons. Although stakeholders will complain if they don't see you included, you will probably get better results by placing your advertisement in a different section of the same newspaper. This situation varies from media market to media market.

The stronger and more established your brand name, the more effective your overall marketing program. The greater power your name has in the marketplace, the more important you become. Marketing becomes easier as your brand becomes more influential.

Radio, TV, and cable can be effective for branding, but, since saturation is very important, cost quickly becomes a factor. Are you in a market that considers advertising for your school to be a public service announcement (PSA) and therefore entitled to free time? If so, your only cost is the production of the spot. But this too can be costly, and a branding spot must impressively clarify your competitive advantage. No spot is better than a poor one. And then, of course, a PSA might not be run very often or get stuck in very low audience schedule times. If you have to pay for time and production, then budget is your whole issue. If you can do it, great; if not, a mix of other media plus word-of-mouth can do the job.

Branding slides at movie theaters puts your name in front of young people and families. Billboards can work very well if they look impressive and are well placed. This goes for bus cards and bus bench cards as well. And don't overlook company newspapers, a very good target market available for very low cost.

Be careful about Web advertising. Millions of people are online and often they are the right target markets. But banner advertisements come and go hit-and-miss on the screen. And it is unclear how people react to them. Take into account frequency, audience, and cost. Make it a cost-benefit judgment and, if you buy banners, try to track your results.

Participation in events and projects are also effective branding activities. Some of these include

- Community arts and holiday events
- Conferences, meetings
- Lecture series
- Open houses
- City and neighborhood initiatives
- Public school events
- Special media projects, i.e., community forums, health fairs

In some cases you may be putting on the event or initiating the project. In other cases you may be co-sponsoring the event. In still others you may be only a sponsoring advertiser.

But in all cases you have a good opportunity to be visible and to reinforce your brand. Pick events and projects that match your institutional strengths and institutional niche. And remember that within each target market you are aiming to interact with the opinion leaders and stakeholders.

A FINAL WORD ON BRANDING

It is important to remember the power of the spoken word in developing a brand. Top executives who look like they know what they are doing are powerful agents of branding. Leaders telling the story with conviction have a powerful emotional impact, which influences the development of brand perceptions. "Walking the talk" means doing as well as saying.

The word-of-mouth communication that follows is equally powerful. That is why direct communication with stakeholders and opinion leaders is an important branding tool. There is an emotional communication impact when respected people in the community are saying, "Look what's going on out at the university!" And that romances the brand in very powerful ways.

Which brings up the subject of consistency. There is always a tendency to change messages and designs. The thought is that people become bored with them. But people who work with them become bored with them far sooner than do the audiences. In fact, the point where you think you can't stand to hear it or see it again may be when the message is just beginning to get through to your audience. This is especially true from the perspective of branding.

In order to develop a brand, you need to be consistent over a sustained period of time with your use of logo, overall design and look, tag line, and supporting messages. Three or four years down the line you might gradually change to demonstrate growth and relevance to a changing world. But do that very carefully and skillfully, making certain to repeat and repeat and repeat the essence of the brand. One thing for sure: A new tag line to kick off every year is *not* what you need.

CHAPTER TWELVE

Marketing Admissions

There was a time when professionals could with fair accuracy predict enrollment. Indicators from previous years would be fairly reliable. Experienced admissions deans could predict how many students would actually show up on campus based on admitting a larger number of prospects who fit a historical profile. An unknown element existed only if the institution was trying to attract students outside the profile—smarter students, minorities, students from a completely new geographic region. Even then, the risk factor could be controlled by limiting how many of those were actually expected to show up.

But then the world changed for many institutions, gradually at first, then rather dramatically. Suddenly, admissions offices realized that their predictors were no longer very reliable. Students were applying to more institutions. More and more students were paying additional application fees just to be able to have a choice later in the game. Many students learned they could negotiate financial aid with some institutions, especially if they were very bright and the institution needed them. Some of these negotiations took place pretty late in the summer, changing the whole process. Some would even attend orientation on several campuses late in the summer before they made a final decision. The institution would not know their choice until they actually showed up.

INTEGRATED MARKETING AND ADMISSIONS

As admissions departments became arenas of uncertainty, new ideas were needed to address the situation. One place to look was the field of integrated marketing, which provided a systemic way of analyzing the marketplace. It championed the use of target research to explain the change more clearly. It advocated mobilizing the total institution to address the problem. It favored the formation of teams made up of all of the talented marketing and communications people on campus to focus on institutional priorities. It also adapted the latest thinking in corporate marketing to the academy, with a special concern not to compromise the academy's integrity by commercializing it.

After forming an institution-wide task force or steering committee or some other official planning group to guide the project, the first step is to set some institutional goals. These goals, in one way or another, almost always call for more visibility and more and better applications for undergraduate admission. In order to eventually produce a plan or blueprint for action, the first step is to evaluate the current admissions operation.

COMMUNICATION AUDIT AND RESEARCH

Begin with a communication audit. I discussed the audit process in the chapter on research (Chapter 7). It is always a very enlightening exercise to lay out all of your admissions materials, publications, letters, postcards, etc., note where in the process other communications take place, and perform a content analysis to determine their effectiveness. You are analyzing for consistency of competitive-advantage message, family look and design, timing and interactive opportunities. Once done, the materials audit usually reveals very obvious places to make improvements. Often the auditing process leaves the group feeling that all of the materials need to be re-done in a reasonably short period of time.

Most institutions budget admissions materials to be re-done every two years. If this is the case, and it is possible to make sure the key ones are done first, then it will be possible to stay on that schedule. It might not take new money, just a lot of time and effort on the part of your most creative and imaginative task force members. But improvements in consistency, intensity, and, ultimately, impact of materials and other communications will produce results.

As you prepare new materials, take your priority market segments into account. Therefore you will need to go through the exercise of identifying them and learning about their needs and aspirations. This no doubt means doing some targeted survey research, which was also discussed in Chapter 7. An analysis of individual market segments and associated research will show where you need to focus your messages. Many materials will work for all segments if you target special interests in a cover letter or other enclosures. For other market segments, such as parents or minorities, you may need to produce some special materials.

Some institutions are considering the development of separate materials and communications for each target market, a theoretically desirable but very expensive undertaking. Also, digital printing technology, coupled with the Internet, provides some interesting new segment—and in some cases individual—targeting. But many of these technical bells and whistles backfire because, even in a digital world, the ultimate appeal is the personal relationship. Personalization achieved through technology can actually feel impersonal. Since it's all in the execution, evaluation of each tactic is essential.

MARKET SEGMENTATION AND MEDIA PREFERENCES

The communication audit requires you to first identify your priority market segments so that you can evaluate their impact as you consider their special characteristics. This is true about media preference as well. As stated in Chapter 7, several research companies perform periodic studies of admissions media preferences in general. Once you identify your target markets, you can also find out each segment's preferences.

An analysis of media preference by market segment will potentially change the mix of materials you send each one, still another level of sophistication that can have cost implications. Focus on your primary segments and get them right. The more focused and more interactive, the more effective your effort will be.

A list of general preferences can be helpful, but this list changes. For example, even after the saturation of the Internet, the picture catalog, or viewbook, has long ranked number one in overall preference. However, the Web site is now first on many lists. No matter what is number one or two, they are all a part of a mix, and the total impact of the mix is what matters most.

... even after the saturation of the Internet, the picture catalog, or viewbook, has long ranked number one ... the Web site is now first on many lists.

The primary media in student recruiting, listed in an approximate order of general preference, include

- The Web
- Viewbook
- E-mail
- College guides
- Personal letters
- Academic program brochures
- Co-curricular services brochures
- Telephone calls
- Campus visits
- College nights
- High school visits
- Application form

There is, however, an even longer list of what might be called secondary media that provide a lot of creative opportunity. They are as effective as they are creative, and they must play a strategic impact role in the total mix. If they stand out and have impact, they can distinguish you from other institutions and reinforce your emotional presence, or brand. You will generally not use a lot of these, but rather select them based on your market segment research. Secondary media include

- Videos
- CD-ROMs
- Audio tapes or CDs
- Newsletters
- Magazines
- Posters
- Postcards/flyers
- Special events/dinners/receptions
- Admissions seminars
- Print advertising
- Electronic advertising
- TV and radio public service announcements (PSAs)
- News media placement
- Mailings/calls to parents
- Alumni calls
- Focus groups, interviews, surveys

Videos can be mailed directly to prospective students or used for emotional impact at meetings and events. Ironically in this the television age, videos sent to the home are often not opened. Some money formerly spent on videos is being diverted to the Web.

CD-ROMs present the same problem as videos. Often those sent to the home are not used. Prospective students seem to be going directly to the Web. Some professionals think that a CD-ROM inserted into the viewbook is a good transition medium, a way to transport the viewer/reader from print publication to CD-ROM to the Web. And an audio CD or tape can be effective when the institution's jazz band or other entertainment group is the content sent as a gift.

Events ... are of special importance to integrated marketing, especially for student recruiting, because of the relationship-building potential.

A special periodic newsletter can make prospective students feel they are already on campus and that the campus is an exciting place to be. But unless newsletters are carefully edited to generate this sense of excitement, they can backfire. Some institutions just send prospective students their magazine, but a follow-up readership evaluation is advised. The concern is that most of these magazines are edited for an alumni audience and, therefore, students throw them away without reading them.

Postcards and novelty gifts can be effective. They have a special impact when they arrive, and they help with timing. You can pick those times in the sequence of mailings to fill in a timing gap. Some have found institutional T-shirts to be effective. If you can get a prospect to wear your identity, the result can be psychologically powerful and the prospect becomes a walking billboard.

Events, as discussed previously, are of special importance to integrated marketing, especially for student recruiting, because of the relationship-building potential of any interactive moment. Some schools hold receptions or dinners in cities around the country where current students, faculty, staff, and alumni can meet with prospective students and parents. Others hold admissions seminars to help prospective students and parents understand the admissions process, irrespective of what school they finally decided to attend. The theory here, of course, is that they are likely to attend an institution with which they already have relationships.

Both producers and consumers give TV and radio advertising and PSAs mixed reviews. Some spots seem to work, others clearly do not. There is no consistent rule of thumb. Radio seems to work for low-cost institutions such as junior colleges that register students who make very-last-minute decisions. That is assuming that they buy or are given enough time to get sufficient saturation. Both radio and television seem to require a sustained presence to have impact. Some institutions have found that a television spot with enough saturation to clarify identity and enhance visibility can be an effective part of a media mix. But expense is a real issue here, and many stations are making less and less free time available for these kinds of announcements.

Alumni and current parents can be helpful in student recruiting. So can sending press clips and news releases directly to prospects when the topics are of interest or especially impressive. A focus group or survey or interview is a two-way communication opportunity. In addition to receiving information, you have a real opportunity to send messages as well. Always state and reinforce your brand when you introduce any research project.

When it comes to content and layout of materials, integrated marketing experience and research suggest some considerations. Stunning photography is clearly worth the extra money. Most institutions settle for too-little quality in a world dominated by dramatic pictures. You must compete with the best media around to be effective. The pictures should mostly depict people with exciting backgrounds. An attractive campus and buildings in the background are important for providing atmosphere, but prospects project themselves into the picture and want to see people like themselves in it. Design needs consistently reinforce your identity but mildly reflect current trends in the details. Good designers know how to do this. A prospective student doesn't want an academic institution to look like MTV, but the materials should suggest that the institution is savvy about the world around it. The competitive advantage message needs to be up front and clear, and the rest of the text needs to be concise, easy to skim, and interactive in tone. When read aloud, a written piece should sound inviting and conversational. When heard, a radio script should be crisp and to the point. A TV spot should illustrate the message in pictures, reinforced only by the sound. If it's a talking head, it better be a good one.

The total impact and overall tone of communication is critical to success. You should never evaluate a medium standing alone. Rather see it for its role in the total mix, and evaluate the composite intensity, timing, and impact.

INFORMATION AT HAND

Do not begin with the information you have but rather with the information you need. One of the biggest mistakes made in marketing is to gather all of the information you can and then try to analyze it. You will be impressed with all the information you have at hand but get confused trying to make sense of it. You may already have most of what you need, so determine the need before you gather it. You don't need a lot of information, but you do need the right information.

Begin with a basic profile of the current campus population by gender, age, ethnicity, zip code, grades, class rank, test scores, and activities. Set up your computer system to track applications coming in the categories that mean the most to you on a weekly or even daily basis to determine the location of more students who have the characteristics you seek. Research companies can provide their zip codes. Then decide how to communicate with them. Research can ascertain their needs. The tracking is ongoing so the database keeps building.

REEVALUATING POLICIES

Critical policies determine when you offer admissions, how firmly you require a commitment from students, your application and housing fees, how and when you process financial aid, and when and how you will make exceptions to your standards. Remember that prospects talk to other prospects, so your procedures have to be consistent. Too many exceptions in one high school, for example, can destroy your credibility for years.

There are competitive reasons for reconsidering these policies, however. You might want to consider admitting students earlier but requiring a firm commitment from them. You might want to drop admissions standards but require more people to take remedial workshops. You might want to allocate your financial aid differently, perhaps to attract more males or students who have leadership potential but lower test scores. These are important considerations, and in a changing marketplace there are no standard procedures any more. You will have to experiment, measure your results, and resolve to change several times.

MORE FEEDBACK IN THE SYSTEM

Because constant feedback helps you modify what you are doing as you go along, you should be seeking feedback in almost every communication. Enclose return cards, distribute evaluation forms, ask questions in conversations, and make every communication an opportunity to learn or evaluate something.

Make the office environment a place for feedback. While people are waiting for an interview with a counselor, have them fill out a brief questionnaire. Make it brief and colorful, but don't *require* them do it. Just tell them you are interested in their ideas. Conclude office interviews with a few questions about needs and opinions.

Also, train the travel team of recruiters to bring back information from high school counselors, students, and parents. Give them each the same questionnaire to carry on calls, so that the information they collect will be comparable and vitally useful. It is an extremely effective way of staying on top of a changing marketplace.

Don't force a long questionnaire on anyone. To make this feedback approach work, tell people that you really care what they think, make it comfortable for them to answer questions, and ask only a few questions. You don't want to make this a burden, rather you want them to feel flattered that you care enough to ask.

OPENING NEW SEGMENTS

The most effective way to solve an enrollment decline problem is to find more students similar to the students you already have. There are reasons why they chose your school, just as there are reasons why others did not. It always takes more time, more effort, and more money than you think to recruit new kinds of students. That is why the profiling approach described earlier is effective. You profile the students you have and ask an outside research group to provide the zip codes of others like them.

You can also get zip codes for desirable students you do not now attract. There are reasons why these people are not already on your campus. You need to determine those reasons and develop a reasonable strategy to compensate. Again, research can help.

There are some trend factors to consider. First, students tend to go to schools within 500 to 700 miles of home, so they need a compelling reason to buck that trend. Because males in greater numbers prefer larger campuses, more females than males are enrolled in smaller private universities. Males will need a compelling reason to buck that trend.

Minorities tend to go to schools that already have larger numbers of minorities. Hispanics tend to stay close to home. The only way to change any of this is to build strong relationships between the institution and the outside minority communities. Merely hiring a minority recruiter with financial aid and a quota will not work. Multicultural marketing requires the use of minorities, but it also requires a genuine relationship-building effort with the whole community long before the sale is closed.

Do you want better students or just different kinds of students? Where are they? What do they think they need? How can you best interact with them? How long must you work at it, and what will it cost? Are the potential results worth the time and money?

Sometimes it's a far smarter marketing decision to learn to like your current customer rather than try to attract a new kind. It is common for most institutions to think they are dissatisfied with the clients they serve and to constantly search for better ones. But in education there is a noble calling for any way you define your student body and, through marketing analysis, more and more institutions are finding that it's harder to change that market than they thought.

THE ISSUE OF QUALITY

In education, as in many industries, quality is the only thing that sells. If your institution is inexpensive you cannot say, "Well, you got what you paid for." This raises some serious issues, however. How do we define quality? How do we make sure we deliver it? If our brand is our promise, how do we make sure we keep our promise?

Traditionally, many in education have defined quality has as selectivity. The more academically selective you are, the higher your quality, pure and simple. That defines your raw material, but it doesn't describe the production process or the product you produce. And marketing analysis, as well consumer behavior, requires you to address all those other dimensions quickly. And even the first dimension, selectivity, is usually defined on only one dimension—academic performance.

Marketing analysis leads one to conclude that every institution in the world wants the same few students, the academically gifted. All institutions behave as if they attract a good number of them, and they all act dissatisfied with less-gifted students. This presents a marketing dilemma. The market for students everyone wants is very small. The larger market is academically competent but not gifted, and the only way to attract the gifted is with financial aid. Few institutions can survive financially if they continue to think they can attract great numbers of the gifted. And if they continue to behave as if they are achieving this, the new sophisticated consumer will not believe them.

What's more, the new consumer is really interested in other dimensions of the quality issue. Who teaches the students? How big are the classes? How much personal attention do students get? Who will become their mentors? What kind of technology is available? What will they be able to do when they graduate? Can the institution find them a job? All these questions define the quality areas of greatest consumer interest. The institution will have to answer these questions with credibility. Marketing analysis doesn't cheapen the academy, it challenges it to face its realities and to deliver the kind of quality that the consumer values.

Which is not to say that the consumer does not value prestige. And to the degree that level of selectivity establishes level of prestige, the consumer will be interested in selectivity. But as higher education deals with an increasingly sophisticated consumer, the credibility issue for many institutions will get considerably more serious. More and more institutions will be

Marketing analysis doesn't cheapen the academy, it challenges it to face its realities and to deliver the kind of quality that the consumer values.

trying to remain selective by broadening their definition of it. As they define their niche more precisely, they will begin to claim selectivity by matching their more broadly defined definition to what it takes to succeed at their particular kind of institution.

This approach to broadening selectivity introduces a long list of potential factors, and it will take more time to make the judgments. Some of this information is available from high school records and test scores, but other information has to be gathered by interviewing and making judgments about motivation and interests. A list of these factors includes "hard factors" and "soft factors."

Hard Factors

- Grades
- Choice of courses
- Test scores
- Class rank
- School quality
- Group memberships/leadership
- Work experience
- Hobbies
- Family income
- Family education history
- Geographic location/zip code
- Gender
- Ethnicity
- Religion
- Country of origin
- Special talents

Most data on hard factors can be gathered on forms and questionnaires and processed by computer. The soft factors are a bit more difficult to assess, but they may become increasingly important in making admissions judgments. As in hiring staff, prospects' attitudes, judgments, motivations, and creativity can be more important in some campus settings than what they know or even the amount of their experience.

Soft Factors

- Positive outlook
- Creative expression
- Communication skills
- Social skills
- Personal goals
- Sophistication/judgment/savvy
- Beliefs/values/complexity
- Personal style
- Level of motivation

Many of these soft factors will be deemed inappropriate, and others will be added. But the intent is to further define niche through a more precise description of what makes this particular institution selective and why that selectivity is appropriate to the kind of education it delivers. In that way an institution maintains credibility, more precisely defines its competitive advantage, and is eventually able to claim to be the best there is at what it does.

Also consider the impact of perceived relationships on judgments of quality. There is a lot of evidence that, once people develop what they consider a meaningful relationship at an institution, they begin to think that the whole place is better. The power of relationship building is important in every facet of marketing.

GETTING CONSIDERED VERSUS CLOSING THE SALE

In integrated marketing, analysis makes it very clear that different messages matter at different stages of the process. Your materials and communications need to be appropriate for the time they are received. Academic reputation is very important in the process. Even mediocre students want to believe that academic reputation was a major reason they considered a particular school. Over-all visibility and branding initiatives should take this into account. Your competitive advantage, even if it's a convenience or experiential factor, needs to be presented in the context of educational quality. If you can't claim academic quality with some level of credibility, you will have trouble getting considered by any student in the future.

Once you are in a group of schools being considered, other factors determine the final choice. Sometimes it's a perception of convenience. You are close to home. It is easy to commute to class. The residence hall is comfortable. The food service has attractive options. It is possible to exercise close to where I will live. But the most important factor of all is, "I like the people I met when I visited the place."

More often than not, the final decision is based on relationships and the place that was experienced when the visit took place—the "experienced place" as opposed to the place that was seen. The decision is really made because of a relationship with a faculty member who expressed sincere interest, a counselor who offered some personal attention, other students who helped answer questions, or the admissions counselor who took the time to care all these many months.

In this age of high technology and personalized e-mail messages, the campus visit still matters more than any other part of the recruiting process. In the end, it is perceived meaningful relationships that make the real difference. The whole process should be imagined as an interactive dialogue with lots of feedback every step of the way.

FOCUS ON SPECIAL INITIATIVES

Since most admissions professionals are highly experienced and skilled at what they do, when you introduce integrated marketing into the institution it is important to respect their talent and abilities. While the whole process begins with an audit of admissions operations, the intent must clearly be to fine tune what is already being done and then to launch new initiatives that add focus, feedback, and intensity. It expands their team and brings new resources, but it must never usurp their role in managing their own day-to-day work.

Give the admissions office veto power over any new idea. Consult them every step along the way. They will rarely exercise their veto because they will be influenced by the talent and creative new thinking of the strategists, designers, writers, and others on the integrated marketing team. The marketing analysis may generate new ideas that they never thought about, but they are still your best experts on the marketplace itself. Work very hard to keep them in that role. If there is some incompetence in the operation, let the process reveal it over time. Experience teaches that with this kind of teamwork people cannot avoid discovering their own strengths and weaknesses, and they usually select themselves in or out as time goes on.

CHAPTER THIRTEEN

Integrated Marketing and Fund Raising

Professionals in fund raising know better than anyone else in institutional marketing the power of relationship building. In fact, the others would do well to learn this aspect of the business from them. What then can integrated marketing offer fund raising?

EVERYONE'S JOB

The integrated marketing process implemented through institution-wide teams and task forces has the potential to teach everyone about fund raising—what they should and should not do to raise money. The ultimate idea behind integration is that it gets everyone on the same page, not only with respect to a shared understanding of competitive advantage but also with respect to establishing that everyone is responsible for finding students and raising money.

That doesn't mean that people all over campus should go out and ask for money. On the contrary, the integrated process clarifies fund-raising policies on a much wider scale. It rather means that everyone should understand the need to find resources, explain to the people they meet why fund raising is important in education, recognize people of means when they meet them, and give the right people in the fund-raising office information about funding sources. In other words, the more knowledgeable everyone becomes, the better the whole system works.

In addition to learning just how much of a student's education donors pay for, why certain names appear on buildings, how scholarships work, and more, task-force conversations make it clear why individuals should not ask for money without development-office help. They learn the importance of knowing individual donors' giving histories before making another ask. They learn that donor research helps prevent asking for too little or asking for the wrong project. They learn just how professional development work operates and thereby increase their appreciation of it. They also learn how satisfying it can be to cultivate a gift when it is done with professional support.

THE PASSION FACTOR

The stronger the brand name and emotions associated with it, the more effective all aspects of marketing will be, including fund raising. A brand name may be particularly emotional because it inspires great achievement or suggests a cause of special importance in the minds of consumers. We sometimes call this the "passion factor."

The greater the passion factor, the easier the fund raising. Donors still need projects of interest and tangible activities to support. But when those solicitations are made in an atmosphere of a passion for the cause, the whole process is more effective and rewarding. The integrated marketing process can play a major role in enhancing the passion associated with the brand.

OTHER MOTIVATIONS FOR GIVING

Research associated with integrated marketing clarifies the needs and interests of market segments. Therefore, addressing special interests directly becomes a focus of the integrated process, meeting consumers where they are with respect to their known interests and then taking them beyond those initial interests as the relationship matures. The relationship is established based on interests.

This dimension that marketing brings to development can broaden the way it goes about its daily work. The tendency has been to appeal to the egos of donors with recognition, and then move them from one giving level to another with promise of greater recognition. This is an important aspect of the process, and experience teaches that it works. But these ego appeals can be immeasurably enriched with programs that also involve them in aspects of the institution related to their special interests.

MARKET SEGMENTS AND MEDIA PREFERENCES

Do you identify donor market segments by gift level, by age, by geographic location, or by special interests? The best answer is all of the above, and how you do it changes from circumstance to circumstance. But special interests play an increasingly important role.

Knowing media preferences for donor-market segments is critical as well. For example, some people dismiss newsletters as items that everyone throws away without reading. But research indicates that, in some fund-raising contexts, a well-edited and well-laid-out newsletter is the most effective of all fund-raising materials. As in all marketing, the right mix of focused media is the most effective.

- Fund-raising-related media
- University magazine
- Donor newsletter
- Giving report
- Direct mail solicitation
- Web presence
- Dinners, receptions
- Programs, entertainment
- Alumni club activities
- Continuing education, lectures
- Campus visits, tours

A well-edited and attractive donor newsletter can be very effective. Its immediacy in reporting gifts and givers, coupled with discussions of donor interests and donor recognition, can be quite powerful. The proof, of course, is in the details, because a badly done newsletter can be deadly and counterproductive. The university magazine has similar potential, but its strength is to place the major donor stories in the context of the whole university.

The giving report, which lists every donor by giving level, is a bit controversial. Its proponents argue that donors look for their name and are motivated by seeing their name and the names of others in print. Other professionals think that, given the time and effort it takes to produce them, these reports are not cost-effective enough. Experience tends to go both ways. A well-done report has positive impact, but it has to be well done. If it's a choice between a donor report and a newsletter, a well-done newsletter should probably win out.

Direct mail is an important part of any fund-raising program, but integrated marketing broadens the context to include any direct and interactive media that reach target markets and add new content. The Web is an increasingly important part of the mix; it includes e-mail when you know the address you have is used. But when you see donors as stakeholders and understand the power of the passion factor, direct communications should not just be solicitations. They should also include all kinds of reports, news clips, invitations, and more that relate to donor interests.

Fund raisers know how to do special events. This is another place marketers in other areas can learn from them. And as in admissions, sales are closed based on real experiences of the place. Every special event should communicate the brand and the emotion. Every event should have a communications objective, a setting that reinforces it, and opportunities for feedback and relationship building. Never just throw a party. This includes dinners, receptions, fine-arts programs, alumni activities, continuing-education courses, campus visits and tours, and any enticement to gather people together.

STRATEGIC INITIATIVES

Integrated marketing, through its institution-wide processes, can add focused initiatives to donor cultivation. When deans and academic departments participate in conversations about finding students and money, they become more motivated to help. It becomes more and more possible over time to involve them in cultivating donors. Academic departments can include donors on mailing lists, invite them to academic activities, and even seek their opinions about professional trends. Some donors are very qualified to speak in classes, and most consider it a bonding experience. The more donors feel connected to the core business, the more their passions soar.

Special-interest groups can be formed as donor interests become clarified. A technology group or a history group or an art group or a theater group—the list of potential special-interest groups is endless. Once initiated, these groups can be somewhat self-sustaining, using Internet chat rooms and volunteers to schedule periodic meetings.

CAMPAIGN COMMUNICATIONS

Integrated marketing analysis suggests that if the case for a comprehensive fund-raising campaign is developed in the right way, everyone involved in that campaign will know that case by kickoff without ever reading the materials. The key is to design an integrated process that involves all the right people from the very start of planning.

The initial objectives are to locate and qualify donors as well as to define, identify, locate, and qualify potential donors. But from the beginning, a key strategic objective is also to make donors and potential donors feel a close relationship to the institution and want to take responsibility for its future. The way pre-campaign activities are organized and managed is critical to achieving these objectives.

PRE-CAMPAIGN ACTIVITIES

Wherever possible, a total institutional strategic-planning project should precede a campaign. Such a project should be highly participatory, making key constituents feel ownership of the institution's future. An integrated marketing program can lead the institution into such a project, which in turn can lead into a campaign. How strategic participatory planning can be organized and implemented will be addressed in Chapter 17. Suffice it to say here, such a project can move marketing to the next level of effectiveness and set the stage for a highly motivated campaign.

When campaigns are being planned, the initial step is a feasibility study. This is where all the needs and aspirations that come from institutional planning are tested with key donors to determine their level of interest as well as commitment. Here is where the interests of the institution must be translated into the interests of donors. The communication aspect of this process is very important. It is not just a questionnaire that must be filled out, but a passion that needs to be ignited and a feeling of connection that must be consummated.

Next comes the development of the case itself. Based on the results of the feasibility study, the needs of the organization are organized to appeal to donor interests. The best approach is to develop a case outline and involve the people who will have to make it work in a discussion. Visit volunteers one-on-one. Hold roundtables in major geographic locations to discuss the case. Use alumni gatherings, as well as gatherings of parents, staff, and faculty, to discuss the case. Gradually expand the outline into a draft, and then circulate the draft for more discussion.

Along with producing a sense of ownership for the campaign, this process gets the people involved to memorize the case. When the printed case statement finally appears, few people involved with the campaign will actually have to read it. Rather, it becomes a symbol of the campaign, a tool that people carry with them and leave behind. It is an important symbol and needs to be produced. But the case will be made not by the printed piece, but by the passion of the people.

The case statement is the centerpiece around which other materials revolve.

CAMPAIGN MATERIALS

As in all marketing, the materials support the leadership and rhetoric of the people, they do not carry the campaign. It is important to keep that role for them in mind when you are producing them. And it is important to involve and train volunteers accordingly. They lead; materials support.

Types of Campaign Materials

- Case statement
- Campaign newsletter
- Video
- Project proposal/papers
- Volunteer manual
- Pledge card
- Web site
- CD-ROM
- E-mail newsletter
- Audio CD
- Volunteer giveaways (T-shirts, pens, etc.)
- Donor recognition gifts (plaques, paperweights, bookends, etc.)

The case statement is the centerpiece around which the other materials revolve. As a symbol, its look and emotional impact is important. It establishes graphics standards that then become consistent in subsequent pieces. The campaign logo and tag line need to be compatible with the institution's logo and tag line. Consider the campaign a sub-brand, like athletics or the business school, that needs its own identity but must connect with and reinforce the institution's identity.

The campaign newsletter should become the most important piece of support communication. It reports results, establishes and maintains a sense of momentum, and rewards donors soon after they make gifts. Donor stories, if well written, can motivate others to get involved. The key is to communicate their feelings, their satisfactions, their passions. Put enough time, talent, and money into this to make it really attention-getting and interesting.

A video should not be just another version of the case statement. If you do a video, make it something else. It should be compatible with the printed case statement, working with but not duplicating it. Imagine the case statement on the table at a dinner and the video as the experience that will motivate someone to pick it up. The video can include testimonials from prior donors, statements of passion from current volunteers, or histories of what philanthropy has accomplished in the past. It should not be a narrated list of needs.

Specific papers describing projects, volunteer manuals that detail procedures and dates, and easy-to-understand pledge cards are important support materials as well. CD-ROMs and audio CDs are less important; they are taken but often not used. E-mail newsletters are as good as their addresses, but they can be very effective if your donors are wired. Build your address list carefully, and use it to the extent that you can.

Volunteer giveaways and donor recognition gifts can be very important—not so much because they motivate giving, but because they serve as billboards and help "brand" the campaign. Campaign visibility, as in other aspects of marketing, is more important within market segments than in the community as a whole.

OTHER SUPPORT COMMUNICATIONS

Integrated marketing brings together elements of the whole institution to set goals and work to achieve them. This benefits a campaign too. When the institution is in a campaign, the task force can turn attention to its support.

This support includes all members of the communications staff as well as its strategic thinkers, writers, designers, events people, sports marketing, and more. The reputation-defining stories selected for pitching to the news media will provide background for areas addressed in the campaign. Occasionally, a campaign story might get news coverage, i.e. the kickoff event or a really major gift. But the biggest support will be in terms of editorial judgment. Gradually, the topics in the case statement will be reinforced in the press and elsewhere by stories that support them.

This will happen with communications to stakeholders and opinion leaders as well, and not just with those who are donors. The marketing and communication office can send press releases, news clips, copies of advertisements, and more that support and reinforce campaign goals directly to key word-of-mouth supporters.

This reinforcement materializes in the way the magazine is edited during a campaign, in the selection of topics for institutional advertising, and in virtually all other communications. That is the benefit of integrated marketing. Over time, it shows people how powerful a totally orchestrated approach can be.

CHAPTER FOURTEEN

Broadening the Mission of Alumni Relations

When people contemplate integrating the whole institution's marketing activities, the real potential of involving as many alumni as possible in all aspects of marketing and communications becomes very clear. Just as with faculty, staff, students, and parents, getting more alumni involved with raising money, finding students, and building reputation can be very powerful and very cost effective.

Over the years, some development people have come to see alumni work primarily as a way to cultivate donors. It is certainly that, but integrated marketing analysis leads one to realize that alumni can be highly effective student recruiters and their energetic, highly motivated word-of-mouth support can be worth a thousand paid reputation-building advertisements as well. Integrated marketing includes an important broader mission for alumni relations in educational institutions. No matter where it is located on the organizational chart—and even if it is independent from the institution itself—the alumni relations program should set its goals to advance all of the institution's goals and organize its work accordingly. This means broadening its activities and participation.

BROADENING THE BASE

People who are active in alumni activities tend to be those who were socially active while on campus. They were campus leaders who joined clubs and got involved in student government. They attended athletics events and participated in other social activities. Most alumni relations programs are very good at serving their needs.

But where are the rest of the alumni? What about the engineers who had other interests? What about the people in the arts who were always rehearsing? Where are the journalists who spent late nights writing for the campus newspaper? How do we connect with the scientists who spent their time on campus in labs working on experiments? Does the alumni relations program reach out to these people, and is it in the institution's best interests to do so?

Integrated marketing seeks ways to get academic departments and other units involved in broadening the alumni base. Some departments will think about forming their own sub-groups. Others may want only to invite their alumni to events. Some will not respond at all. But over time more and more academics will come to appreciate the long-term benefits of getting more involved. The benefits may be attracting more financial support or finding more good students or even seeing the reputation of the department grow. But to broaden this participation, one needs to broaden the program's objectives and activities.

WORD-OF-MOUTH SUPPORT

People brag about an institution that they strongly admire, usually without being asked. But it can be much more effective if you develop a plan to involve them in discussions of mission, vision, and values, and if you determine what themes best communicate them. Playing a role in this aspect of integrated marketing can, and probably should, become a formal objective and activity of the alumni program.

This can begin at a board retreat and extend to discussion groups in key cities. It can be launched as a formal part of the integrated marketing effort with promises that all ideas will be recorded and presented to the overall task force. The bottom line, of course, is that once the message is clear, individual alumni are officially asked to spread the word. And you can give them materials and fact sheets to help.

Begin by asking alumni to spread the word to opinion leaders and stakeholders. Give them lists of these people along with specific requests to call them or visit to deliver the message. Ask them to send notes. They might break the ice by saying the reason for the visit is to find out what important leaders think. Once the call is made, and the listening has taken place, they can effectively communicate the competitive advantage message. The ultimate message: "This is a new day for this institution. We are going places, and we want you to come along."

Finding Students

On surveys, most students report that they chose to attend an institution because they were influenced by someone who knew it and liked it. This person might have been a parent, family friend, fellow student, or high school counselor. In many cases it was an alumnus, since happy alumni are some of the best student recruiters.

Indeed, while many alumni relations programs are involved in student recruiting, integrated marketing analysis suggests that this activity should be elevated to the status of one of three major goals, along with word-of-mouth communication (reputation building) and fund raising. It is that important to the institution. It helps alumni sustain the very lifeblood of the institution—its students—and it keeps them connected with the core business in a very meaningful way. It is very rewarding to see a student you helped recruit graduate four years later and go on to a successful life.

Set up a special organization within the alumni relations program to coordinate student recruiting. Ask alumni to represent the school at college nights and career fairs. Ask them to give send-off parties in their communities for new students coming to campus for the first time. Ask them to make lists of friends and professional colleagues who have children or know potential students. This organization within an organization does not have to become just a small optional activity, however. Integrated marketing analysis suggests that finding great students for the institution should be a central mission. It's a natural role for alumni, and it clearly makes the place better.

Alumni play a vital role in raising money. Many donors who get their early cultivation through alumni activities later become strong givers.

Raising Money

Alumni play a vital role in raising money. Many donors who get their early cultivation through alumni activities later become strong givers. This is as it should be, and the message of financial stewardship—"Others paid for part of your education, now you should help someone else"—should be delivered early in the alumni experience and even before.

But adding reputation building and student recruiting to the mission of alumni relations only strengthens fund raising. It is these kinds of relationship-building activities, activities that have nothing to do with asking for money, that motivate interest in giving and asking. It comes back to passion and emotional involvement. The more you have of these, the more people will do whatever it takes to make exciting things happen. It is a matter of orchestrating the dynamics as well as organizing activities. In other words, the alumni relations program should play a strong role in building the institution's brand.

Special Interest Groups

Most traditional alumni programs are organized around traditional meetings and events: homecoming, reunions, pre-game parties, club meetings, etc. And these activities are very successful at keeping the traditional alumni actively involved. Nothing should be done to change that because these people have high potential as supporters and donors.

But how many new people might be attracted if they had a chance to meet people with similar special interests or learn more about related special topics? It is possible to float a number of topics out and see what interest develops. People may be interested in jazz, or chamber music, or painting, or art history, or computers, or weightlifting—all topics where the educational resources of the institution could attract new people and keep them involved. And once involved, they eventually can be channeled to help with building reputation, finding students, and raising money.

Using the Internet

Special interests might be served over the Internet. Interested alumni can be asked to sign up for chatrooms on special-interest topics or invited to join a listserv. Introduce many topics to see which ones work. Once conversations begin online, groups can decide whether or not to meet face to face. These groups can be formed with very little involvement of staff. The interest group can be tracked, and someone in the group can organize and lead meetings. Special interests might have ties to academic departments and other units in the school. Faculty, staff, and, in some cases, students can be recruited to serve as resources and to lead meetings.

International Alumni Relations

The Internet can also be a tool to maintain connections with international alumni. For many schools, international alumni activities are not practical because too few alumni are spread across many countries, and these people don't stay in one place very long. And many do not have high fund-raising potential. But special-interest membership can cross foreign boundaries on the Internet. And once connected, alumni can be helpful in many ways, including international student recruiting and building relationships with other international entities important to the future of the institution.

Life-Cycle Marketing

The ultimate challenge of alumni relations is to keep people connected to their alma mater for their entire lifetimes. And if you can include the whole family, then the institution can become self-perpetuating. Establish a program that offers different opportunities as alumni and their families move through different stages of life. First, there are get-togethers for young alumni. Then make continuing education and professional upgrade opportunities available. Then provide opportunities to see friends. Then family and recreational activities come along. Then send a congratulation card when a new baby arrives. Then offer early childhood programs. Then offer recreational sports for kids. Then provide help in picking a college for the kids. Provide retirement planning too. And the cycle goes on.

The whole idea that an educational institution is a resource for a lifetime plays out in an organized way for each and every alumnus. That is life-cycle marketing, and it can keep entire families involved as students, as events supporters, as donors, and as word-of-mouth reputation builders. And in the end, that's integrated marketing.

Getting the Board on Board

For an alumni board, an invitation to become a part of a total institutional marketing effort can be exciting. Most active volunteers will find the experience rewarding, and it can add a whole new dimension to volunteering.

First, volunteers have an opportunity to learn a lot more than they knew about the institution. Second, they come to feel more connected than they did before—not just with old school buddies but with the people who shape academic programs and make their lives inside the academy. And third, they get to broaden their vision of what they can do to serve.

An integrated marketing program makes everyone feel important. Everyone from strategic thinkers to people with design ideas to would-be writers get a chance to contribute ideas. Once the team makes things happen, everyone gets a satisfying feeling of accomplishment. It makes giving money the result of a good experience rather than a pressured obligation of membership. And it offers people more options for what to do with their time.

For all these reasons, alumni boards are likely to respond well to integrated marketing. While at first it seems like a lot more for the staff to do, in the final analysis, if you set priorities and focus on them, what you don't get done is what is least important. Much of what is suggested above is predicated on mobilizing other people—other talented professionals on the institution's marketing task force, other people in academic departments, other staff in special interest areas, and volunteers who will be asked to take on special-interest projects more independently.

CHAPTER FIFTEEN

Rethinking Community Relations

Integrated marketing logic allows an institution to see new reasons for building relationships in the community. Not only can an institution be a vital educational resource, but integrated marketing analysis also suggests that community relationships can leverage visibility, locate new traditional students, and develop new sources of support. In other words, there are important marketing as well as educational reasons to do community relations well. Put aside assumptions that town-and-gown stresses are typical and unavoidable to get the most benefit from integrated strategic thinking.

THE GREATER BENEFITS OF ADULT EDUCATION

Most public institutions have a clear mandate to serve their community with educational programs—which usually means developing ambitious adult continuing-education programs. But private institutions that see their mission as serving traditional students often think that developing close educational ties to the city and region is not within their mission. This is especially true if a lower-cost public institution in the area already serves adults.

I have already made the point that the more narrowly focused the institution's niche and the more narrowly defined its market segments, the more effective the marketing program.

It will at first sound contradictory to suggest that a smaller private institution with a more traditional mission should expand its interests in adult education. But there are a number of reasons why opening or expanding this market segment is a good idea and should be seen as an exception to the rule.

First, you will build your continuing education offerings out of program strengths and resources that are already in place. In other words, you will play to your strengths, not just offer programs. Your intention is to further define your brand not by just offering them courses but by letting the community see what you do well. Second, this adult market will be inclined to respond because local citizens will automatically think it makes sense for you to reach out to them. Third, the benefits to you will then far exceed tuition income. The lasting benefits will be word-of-mouth support and visibility, broader support when you seek funds and partnerships to make other things happen, and a natural growing reputation and prestige.

Adults may be a separate market segment, but serving them is a vital part of an overall philosophy of lifelong learning. Almost all institutions—public and private, large and small—affirm that idea. Serving the adults in your community means only that you will broaden the invitation to participate beyond your alumni and that you will direct your marketing and communication accordingly. In short, this move really doesn't change your mission, and it opens up a lot of new opportunities for building reputation within the region and far beyond.

Educational Opportunities with Marketing Benefits

- Noncredit enrichment courses
- Degree completion opportunities
- Professional update seminars and workshops
- Retraining and new career opportunities
- Liberal arts courses and degrees for professionals

- Contract training
- Speakers and lecture programs
- Intercollegiate athletics

Many institutions feel that noncredit courses in cooking or gardening are not very academic and, therefore, not appropriate to their mission. But, to extend the previous discussion of serving special interests, this is a way to reach people and get them involved. The courses and instruction can and should be of very high quality, and when they are they will attract opinion-leader-level participation. Coming to see the institution as a resource for learning about special interests and meeting other people who share them is a vital long-term relationship-building activity. This activity can certainly lead to taking more courses of all kinds, and it has implications for leveraging visibility and cultivating support far beyond the classes themselves.

Degree completion opportunities are especially important in cities with a large number of industries that hire a lot of people who have done some university work but have not graduated.

Degree completion opportunities are especially important in cities with a large number of industries that hire a lot of people who have done some university work but have not graduated. Giving them a chance to complete their degree at a great institution is a real service to them and to their companies. And again, the benefits extend beyond the educational program itself.

Programs to update people in their chosen field or to retrain them for a new career are especially important in this rapidly changing world. These grow out of your existing program strengths and should be offered by your academic departments as a part of your commitment to lifelong learning. Extending invitations to take these seminars and workshops to others in the community who graduated elsewhere generates a kind of "alumni feeling" with those who respond. And this feeling makes them your advocates in many other ways.

Some of the brightest people in the community have completed their professional education but remain interested in the world of ideas. They may feel they concentrated on degree preparation in business, or law, or medicine but didn't make the most of those required liberal arts courses. Now they are interested in American history or art or music, and they would like to trade watching television for evening courses or even a liberal arts degree program. Because teaching these people can be exhilarating, these courses and programs can attract some of your best faculty. This is a win-win situation all the way around that lets you bond with the graduates of institutions other than your own.

This also holds true for contract training, although it is a little more difficult to offer. Contract training requires a special kind of teaching and a special kind of faculty, but it permits your institution to play a key role in meeting the workforce needs of the community, helping individuals advance in their careers, and providing a vital service to the corporate and nonprofit world. Contract training not only bonds the graduates of other institutions to yours, it cultivates genuine support from CEOs and managers who realize how important your institution is to them. This has positive implications for corporate giving when the fund raisers come to call.

Bringing distinguished speakers to the community adds to the institution's overall prestige. Lecture programs attract the intellectuals in the community who, more often than not, are opinion leaders and community influencers. The more of this kind of programming an institution sponsors, the more relevant and vital it appears to be.

Intercollegiate athletics should also be regarded as a community relationship-building opportunity. If designed and marketed properly, entire families will come to feel that attending the games on your campus is the social thing to do. And because entire families come, younger people grow up seeing your institution as the place to be. As a result, later on they and their friends are more likely to think of this institution as the academic place to be as well. I will discuss more about athletics in Chapter 16.

OTHER WAYS TO SERVE AND BENEFIT

Building a partnership with a city or region can increase visibility and extend the perception of an institution's significance in powerful ways. The more an institution is seen as linked to the well-being and progress of a city or region, the more power and influence it will wield with all of its publics. And when the city is promoting itself to the world, the institution will be carried along into that wider area of recognition.

This is what is meant by "leveraging"—when one partner gets visibility and recognition, the other gets visibility and recognition too. The purpose of community relations is not just to gain prestige and enhance business in the community; the purpose is to ride along with the community as all of its leaders extend it into the world.

Other than adult education, there are at least three other ways an educational institution can serve its city and region. First, it can act as a facilitator of communication for community problem solving and planning. It can host town halls and forums on vital topics ranging from crime to transportation to AIDS to garbage pickup. It can get involved in neighborhood concerns, using its research capabilities to provide needed data, host meetings, and facilitate discussions.

Chapter 17 discusses a model for moving integrated marketing into integrated strategic planning, demonstrating how to involve hundreds of people from inside and outside the institution in planning its future. This same model can be modified for an entire city, and an academic institution could facilitate the process. What better way for an academic institution to ensure its own healthy future than to help the city plan its future and to involve people from all parts of the community in the conversation?

Second, expand the space and attention given to promoting the city in the institution's marketing materials. Depict and communicate museums, downtown attractions, performing arts organizations, nightspots, major businesses, and overall quality of life benefits. Do this in the viewbook you send to prospective students, and devote ample time to this in your videos and CD-ROMs. When you hold receptions and dinners in other cities, have brochures and materials about the city at hand.

Remember the factors that close the sale for a prospective student. Your academic reputation gets you considered, but other lifestyle and convenience factors close the sale. The "remembered experience" of the visit to campus is very influential, but this memory can be enhanced by a positive impression of the city as well. Does the city offer great opportunities for enrichment and recreation? Are there internship opportunities and jobs upon graduation? This is important information for prospective students.

When you do all this, make sure the mayor, other city officials, business leaders, and everyone you talk to knows it. They won't unless you tell them, and they will be surprised and impressed. Sell the city everywhere you go all over the country and world. City leaders will respond in kind.

Third, get involved in the city's key projects and activities. Establish your presence at arts festivals and career fairs. Offer to help the chamber of commerce with its economic development activities. Be willing to travel with them to cultivate businesses in other parts of the country. Get your marketing and communication staff involved with the convention and visitors organization. Promote your institution's museums, arts events, and athletics programs travel destinations, and remember that virtually every academic program and administrative office is tied to a professional association that could bring a convention or meeting to the city.

Getting involved in the sister cities program or the world affairs council or the international economic development office can foster relationships in other countries that result in new students, study-abroad locations, and research and creative activity opportunities for faculty. The possibilities are endless. The key is to leverage these partnerships and relationships into higher visibility, more students, greater financial resources, and other resources.

WHEN THE CITY RESPONDS IN KIND

The more the institution gets involved in the city, the more the city will include it in its promotions as well. The convention and visitors office features the institution more prominently in its materials. The mayor refers to it in speeches. The chamber of commerce refers to it more often in reports and proposals. Museum directors refer to it with pride.

As a result, opinion leaders and others begin to refer students. They suggest your institution more readily to relatives and friends. It becomes the "hot" school, the "in place" to be. New fund-raising opportunities materialize. Those who are investing in a better, more vital city now see investing in your institution as related to that larger cause. Every great city has a great academic institution, and city fathers who see your institution in that way suddenly have a whole new reason to support you. Now you ask for support not just as a payback from alumni or to support an academic program of special interest, but also to help build a better city.

Partners appear for academic program enhancement. One institution enhanced its mathematics and science program education by forging a formal connection to the local science museum. The creative partnership attracted the financial support of the largest corporation in town, something that neither program had done alone. An independent botanical research institute partners with a university biology department to enhance both of their research programs. The university's faculty and students especially benefited from access to the institute's collection.

Even advances in diversity are possible. Minority leaders told one institution that minority communities did not see it as a comfortable place for them. The institution co-sponsored a weeklong minority economic development conference with the city and invited all minority leaders to campus. By the end of the conference, everyone knew each other, an organization was founded to raise money to help minority entrepreneurs, and the foundation was laid for ongoing relationship building between the institution and minority communities. Experience tells us that attracting minority students begins by establishing working relationships with their community and its leaders.

WEARING THE BRAND

Some institutions find that it pays dividends to view their college store as both a campus and community enterprise. Campus stores, whether operated by national chains or independent, sell clothing bearing your name, and the more people who wear your name the more visible you are. A T-shirt is a walking billboard, and when someone puts on your identity they are making both a powerful statement and an individual commitment.

Integrated marketing discussions do not get very far before the power of merchandising is recognized and discussed at length. Then it is realized that the bookstore manager has probably never been involved with overall university marketing and communication planning, and that the situation needs to be changed.

Through the integrated marketing process, both university marketing people and bookstore managers learn from each other. University marketing people learn why the logo cannot appear on every item in the same way and why everything cannot be produced in only the institution's colors. To keep goods moving, the bookstore has to respond to trends instigated by other parts of the fashion world. Consequently, bookstores need a lot of variety on their shelves.

The bookstore manager, however, learns to appreciate how important it is to the branding of the institution that logo and design conform to standards. This leads to discussions about just what items will carry the official "look" and how others can provide the necessary fashion variety without creating designs that look like logos and thereby confuse the branding process.

It also becomes apparent that the more stores that carry your merchandise, the more it will be seen. Getting merchants in the community to stock your items becomes an important objective. Your name on merchandise in airport shops, downtown stores, hotel stores, or wherever you can work it out increases visibility and enhances prestige. But choose locations that don't cut into the profits of your own store, which is now promoted in the community as well as on campus.

Make sure that manufacturers of your merchandise are properly licensed. This does not seem too important until your institution or one of its branded items becomes unusually popular. Anticipating this possibility, make sure someone on your staff is overseeing this process. Maintain quality standards and make sure profits go where they should. You never know when your mascot might become the next Izod alligator.

Whether or not adult continuing education is a formal part of your mission, being active in your community has important reputation-building, student-recruiting, and fund- raising ramifications. Serving the leaders of your community with the best of your educational programming builds relationships that will help you in countless other ways. And when you form a mutually beneficial partnership with your city or region by facilitating future planning or supporting other civic activities, you leverage visibility that will eventually stretch to other cities, the nation, and beyond. When one partner goes places, the other does too. Suddenly, they each tell the other's story.

CHAPTER SIXTEEN

Integrating Athletics

Many institutional administrators complain that the athletics department operates with total independence. It is almost like there are two sides of the tracks. The administration of the institution is on one side, and the athletics people are "over there," with little or no communication between them. When this is the case—as it is in many places—there is little justification for intercollegiate athletics at all. The tail is not wagging the dog; the tail is not even on the dog.

If this situation exists, it simply must be changed. The only justification for intercollegiate athletics is that it can support and advance the academy. It must be a part of the fabric of the institution, and what it does and how it operates must make sense for the institution overall. There must be regular, interactive communication between the administrators with planning everything—from program to price to delivery to promotion—a totally integrated enterprise.

ATHLETICS AS A MARKETING EXPENSE

One university president has remarked, "I see the athletics deficit as a marketing expense." He was serious, and when you think about it that is just what it is. Compared to what it costs other organizations and corporations to achieve regional or national name recognition or to develop a regional or national brand, the expense makes even more sense. It costs millions of dollars to develop national brands, and there are ways to do it other than athletics. But intercollegiate athletics has evolved into an effective way to develop a brand that also has other features and benefits.

Given the state of the news business and the cost of prime advertising, it would take years and years to develop a national identity on a modest budget. The prestige reputations of top-tier academic schools with no athletics visibility have taken several hundred years to evolve. One might be able to do it by spending millions, but success in promoting academic stories to the news media would require a redefinition of news and doing it with advertising alone would cost a fortune. While one might choose to spend that fortune on advertising rather than athletics, doing it with intercollegiate athletics does have residual benefits.

Athletics has historically been associated with education because the idea of a sound mind in a sound body is clearly compatible with the academy.

BENEFITS OF ATHLETICS

Athletics has historically been associated with education because the idea of a sound mind in a sound body is clearly compatible with the academy. To study hard and then play hard has always been a part of academic culture. It originates with intramural athletic competition in which everyone has a chance to participate, and intercollegiate competition evolves from there.

But once athletics becomes intercollegiate, and fan and alumni pressure develops, and then the sports media and broadcast audiences get involved, and related expenses mount, the whole thing threatens to get out of control. Here is where taking an integrated approach to fine tuning objectives and developing messages can make a big difference. The residual benefits are there if you make the most of them.

NAME VISIBILITY

There are few better ways to get your name in the editorial side of the mass media in so many markets so often than through intercollegiate athletics. Every week, win or lose, your name will be visible to millions. And what we know about visibility suggests that the more visible you are, the higher the quality people think you have as an academic institution.

If your name is known in a high school primarily because it appears in the sports pages, the students don't assume that you are primarily a football or basketball school. They just know they have heard of you, and that makes a big difference when your admissions counselor tells your story. People don't think you are a party school because they see your students cheering on television; they just think you are a well-known school. Many equate visibility to quality, and intercollegiate athletics gets you visibility.

CAMPUS VITALITY

There is something about the athletics atmosphere that translates to a feeling of vitality and excitement. Theater events contribute to that. So do music events and art exhibits. But athletics has a special way of making a fall weekend—or a cold winter weeknight or a spring afternoon—feel special. School spirit developed through intercollegiate athletics adds a unique dimension to collegiate tradition. And certainly there is no harm in this fun if the overall enterprise makes sense, and one must admit that the vitality helps bond the campus community.

ALUMNI RELATIONSHIPS

Beginning on campus with their student experience, alumni use athletics as a way to maintain lifelong ties. These ties should include attending fine-arts events and lectures, enhancing special interests, continuing education, and more. But athletics is an important vehicle for remembering campus experiences and feelings, and it involves coming home to campus frequently. It is an unparalleled relationship-building opportunity. Other campus-type ties have their very important role in the mix, but none would be missed as much as athletics. Athletics is a healthy cultivation and recreation tool, and athletics events are opportunities to promote other events on campus.

COMMUNITY RELATIONS

Chapter 15 discussed how strong community relationships can leverage your name visibility and build your reputation beyond your home town. Well-marketed intercollegiate athletics can also be a very important ingredient in building and sustaining community relations. But the marketing effort needs to be integrated so that relationships are formed and a lot of people are involved in making it happen.

When a city adopts an institution's football or basketball program as the "home team," something special happens between town and gown. Depending on the city, the size of the school, and the make-up of the sports market, the adopted sport might be baseball, soccer, hockey, women's basketball, or something else. Whatever it is that works, the result, if cultivated properly, can be a feeling of ownership and a willingness to support and promote the whole institution.

A PART OF INSTITUTIONAL MARKETING

When the people who market the institution work together with the people who market athletics, very good things happen. Athletics themes and messages can be developed that meet athletics' needs and are compatible with the institution's branding themes and messages as well. Designs can be developed that look athletic and yet support the "family look" of institutional marketing materials. Merchandise in the bookstore can be better coordinated, and academic events and programs can be promoted during games and in athletics newsletters and special events.

The key to making integration happen is to have the appropriate formal mechanism in place. The athletics director and/or athletics marketing and communications director should serve on the institution's overall marketing task force. This presence is a critical symbol of the president's expectations. And the benefits should go both ways. In addition to athletics marketing materials being better coordinated, the institution's marketing materials should better explain and promote the total benefits of athletics to overall campus programs and community.

Leadership rhetoric has to be supportive as well. The president should talk about athletics and review its broader benefits more often with faculty, students, alumni, donors, community groups, and anyone else to whom he or she speaks. The athletics director, coaches, and staff should always reference the benefits and how athletics advances the whole institution. It is important that they walk this talk and reinforce the idea that athletics makes sense in the academy only if it provides all of the benefits (most especially academic program promotion), wide visibility, and brand development.

AN ATHLETICS MARKETING TASK FORCE

An athletics marketing task force can be formed as a subgroup of the institution's task force, a symbol to its members of its integrated ties to overall institutional marketing. Because of its community focus, however, that athletics group should be shaped differently from the other task force action groups. Those groups are likely to be small and comprise mostly inside marketing and communication experts. The athletics group, however, is likely to be much larger and have a much broader membership.

The purpose of the athletics task force, beyond coordinating marketing efforts, is to mobilize the community in support of athletics. Therefore, its membership should include the president of the university, appropriate members of the cabinet, key members of the athletics administration, institutional and athletics marketing executives, members of the board of trustees, the mayor and key city council members, executives from the chambers of commerce and tourism bureau, business and nonprofit leaders, key alumni leaders and donors, neighborhood chairs, and anyone else with a following in the community. This committee or task force can be effective with 100 or more people because they will be asked to work in small groups and to help rally the support of the others they represent. The larger group should have regular breakfast or luncheon meetings to report on subgroup progress. These meetings should be well orchestrated to leave everyone feeling excited and upbeat. The dynamics of this group process are central to achieving everyone-on-the-same-page results.

This task force seeks to establish a place in the heart of the community for the athletics program. An overarching theme is that if you attended the institution we are playing this weekend it's all right to cheer for the opponent—but in every other game we are your home team. This idea that the team belongs to the city or region is a central theme of communications and a rallying cry for the task force.

Task Force Subgroups

- Public relations and advertising
- Ticket deals and packages
- Sponsorship opportunities
- Onsite advertising
- Parking lot entertainment
- Pre-game show
- Halftime show
- Telemarketing

The public relations and advertising subgroup would work to establish the home-team theme or to pick another one that reinforces that general idea. This group should include anyone interested in brainstorming communications strategies and ideas plus professionals from campus and community who can take care of writing, designing, and placing materials.

The ticket deals and packages group would work on incentives to attract people to the venue. One especially important package is the family package because an aim of the project will be to get whole families to think that this is the social place to be. You want to have the whole family involved because you hope to use this as a communication opportunity to attract them to other events and maybe even enroll as students.

Group sales will seek to get groups to make attendance a club activity. Tickets will be discounted, the group's name will be displayed on the scoreboard, they will be introduced and asked to stand, their favorite project will be mentioned, and everyone in the group will get a souvenir. And the athletics marketing department may even provide bus transportation, as feasible and necessary. Sometimes this is particularly necessary for youth and elderly groups.

Sponsorship packages may offer high visibility at the event and entertainment benefits to the sponsor. Packages usually include banners or signs in the venue and a corporate tent in which to entertain clients. Additionally, on-site advertising will be sold to those who want the visibility but not the other benefits of sponsorship. Developing the details of these offerings and selling them are the responsibilities of this group.

Some institutions actually organize a carnival on the parking lot for pre-game entertainment. Music groups play, food is sold, and carnival games are available for the kids. Tailgating is encouraged as an attendance incentive for whole families. The considerable work of organizing these activities is the responsibility of this group, which will often work with a professional producer to get it all done.

Subgroups are formed to enhance pre-game and halftime activities. They will book parachutists, fireworks, singing groups, dancers, and a whole array of other features to enrich the game-day experience. Another aim will be to make this a great family outing, win or lose. Everyone will have so much fun that the fans do not focus on winning as their only incentive to return.

The whole idea of integrated marketing is to mobilize the right people to take responsibility for making the right things happen. In the case of athletics, you will want to get the entire community excited and involved, and you will want to have the right leaders and the right experts participate. The important strategy involves the selection of the task force members and the design of the work of the subgroups. Recognize up front that professionals will have to serve with volunteers on the subgroups to ensure that the work gets done. But when organized properly, integrated marketing can increase attendance income at the games and make athletics a more effective marketing and reputation-building arm of the entire institution.

CHAPTER SEVENTEEN

Participatory Strategic Planning: The Next Step

Integrated marketing can go a long way toward improving the effectiveness of your efforts to find students, raise money, and build reputation. It simultaneously establishes the processes necessary for planning programs, pricing, program delivery, and communications. And by mobilizing institutional resources and talent, it gets everyone associated with marketing and communications on the same page. But the full potential of integration is usually not realized because only some, not all, of the right program and service people are included.

Participatory strategic planning, however, provides a model that extends a market-based approach to future planning that involves hundreds of stakeholders inside and outside the institution. While de-emphasizing the "marketing" word, it is nonetheless based on fundamentally sound marketing principles. It can get you beyond any roadblocks erected by key people who still fail to understand the total marketing mix. It aims to truly orchestrate the total institution.

PREPLANNING ACTIVITIES

The Primary Objective

The basic objective of future planning is to take the institution to the next level of distinction. But there are two primary concerns that arise during preplanning: Does that next level need to be defined up front? And will participants ultimately get upset if their ideas are not implemented?

Unless your mission, vision, and values are clear going into a future-planning project, you will spend the entire project clarifying them.

First, participatory strategic planning is really a search for the very strengths and opportunities that will define the institution's next level of distinction, and that search becomes the focus of the participant's work. It is therefore important to recognize up front that this "definition" will become more clear at the end and cannot be defined at the beginning. Second, as long as *many* good things happen, people really don't expect *everything* to get done. If their pet project is overlooked they will be disappointed, but they will still feel excitement about making a real difference.

Clarifying mission, vision, and values. Unless your mission, vision, and values are clear going into a future-planning project, you will spend the entire project clarifying them. That will be one of the first issues raised in group discussion, and then the entire agenda will change. The statement, "We can't do anything until we clarify our mission and vision," will ring so true that everyone will want to do that before they do anything else.

To avoid this problem, clarify your mission, vision, and values as a preplanning activity. Appoint an institution-wide representative group to take on the project, and present the results of their work at the strategic planning kickoff. All participants will then have in front of them a copy of the statements that they can use as guidelines with which to measure suggestions. As suggestions are made, the question can be asked, "Does that really further our mission?"

Other Objectives

As preplanning conversations proceed, these additional objectives will inevitably be mentioned:

- To clarify our special place in higher education and identify what we do best
- To strengthen relationships with our benefactors
- To identify strengths, weaknesses, opportunities, and threats
- To suggest actions that maximize strengths, minimize weaknesses, seize opportunities, and manage threats
- To assess the financial implications of all suggestions

Note that these are fundamentally marketing objectives: to clarify competitive advantage, build key relationships, and develop and support the right programs or products. Indeed, participatory strategic planning is essentially a marketing-based project, but we have now substituted the terminology of "strategic planning." We have changed the terminology so that more people can be comfortable about getting on the train.

Situation Analysis

A situation analysis identifies the trends in higher education that will impact the institution. Some trends will be national, and others market-specific. It is a matter of doing the research necessary to make a report on the most fundamental issues facing us. An internal committee of selected faculty and administration can oversee such a study and then make a report at the first meeting. The chair of the committee should make the presentation, with an executive summary and full report distributed to all the participants.

Basic Assumptions and Guidelines

To keep from getting off track, participants should consider a number of assumptions that should be clarified at the very beginning. Even though this may sound like it imposes restrictions that participants might resent, they usually appreciate being told how to avoid wasting their time. Such assumptions usually involve specific details like the size of enrollment, pricing policy, debt policy, financial requirements for new construction, endowment spending, etc. However, even after being told about these assumptions, people who feel strongly enough may address some of them anyway. And if they do, it is important that you learn how strongly they feel and why.

BASIC INSTITUTIONAL STATISTICS

Develop a set of basic institutional statistics to distribute to all participants. Present them as answers to frequently asked questions. Participants throughout the project will ask basic questions such as “How many international students do you have?” or “What is your minority enrollment?” or “How many students do you have in chemistry?” and it will be important to have the answers on hand.

Perform this preplanning work to get the planning project off to a good start and to avoid false starts. The more issues that could get the discussion off track you anticipate, the more effective the project will be. You can inoculate issues by considering them during preplanning and addressing them at the kickoff.

SELECTING PARTICIPANTS

It is important to give careful consideration to the people you invite to participate. In theory you want every opinion leader and stakeholder in every internal and external target market—alumni, donors, government officials, business people, nonprofit people, media gatekeepers, high school counselors, high school students, prospective and current parents, current students, faculty, professional staff, and support staff. And you want the leadership from all these segments. As a preplanning activity, assemble a committee composed of the most knowledgeable of the institution's stakeholders and supporters and have them go over a list of every advisory board on campus, leaderships lists from other groups in the community, and internal directories. It is important to get all the right people to participate.

Experience teaches that it is possible to handle a total of 500 participants more or less, half selected from inside the institution and half from outside. This might seem uncomfortable or unusual, but it works. At the end of the project, these people will have talked to each other about the most fundamental academic and quality-enhancing issues, and they will have come to better understand each other. It will be the best investment you ever made in the institution's future, and all the people necessary to make it happen will have a stake in making it happen. It's a fund raiser's dream.

ORGANIZING THE PROJECT

Your preplanning should provide the information necessary so that discussion can focus on generating good suggestions. With preplanning information in hand, identify the subgroups or task forces you need to create in order to address the right issues. In the participatory planning model, consider two kinds of task forces: horizontal and vertical.

Horizontal Task Forces

Horizontal task forces address institutional-wide issues, including

- Total undergraduate experience
- Role of graduate education
- Global programs and influence

- Technology
- Distinctive programs and new directions
- Community and strategic alliances
- Alumni and donor relationship building
- Role of athletics

There may be others you will want to consider. This list must be institutionally specific and reflect what came out of preplanning discussions and committees.

The task force looking at the total undergraduate experience is particularly important for private schools that claim to deliver a unique and special experience. If education is more than a collection of courses, can we clarify it and then improve on it? The future identity of many of these institutions may depend on this more than anything else, and having 500 stakeholders understand it better can be extremely helpful. From a marketing perspective, this group is really talking about niche, competitive advantage, and the importance of branding.

The group considering the role of graduate education is also important for those institutions that are primarily undergraduate. Can you afford graduate programs? If so, how big a program offering is right? And what quality level in what programs can you really achieve? Again, are all of these critical product-related marketing questions?

The task force looking at global programs is critical because global programs have many financial implications. What does being global really mean? Is it an attitude among faculty? Can you achieve it by making sure all courses have international content? If so, how do you achieve it? How much foreign presence can we afford to have? In what parts of the world do we have expertise? Again, all of these questions have serious marketing implications.

How can you afford to keep up with technology? This group has to deal with reality. They may discover the contradiction that, while the institution's technology is already out-of-date, the technology it already has is not nearly used to its potential. What do you do about faculty members who teach in state-of-the-art classrooms with technology they never use? Marketing says that your brand is your promise. Are you delivering on your technology promises?

The group that searches for distinctive programs to improve and foundation strengths that can breed new programs is of critical importance to future planning. While marketing teaches that programs should connect to a need in the marketplace to succeed, it also teaches that quality demands that you focus on what you do well. Don't create programs based only on market need, but rather search for the match between market needs and institutional strengths. This simply has to be an outcome of the planning process, and is a fundamental marketing concern.

It is clear from the previous discussion of community relations how important the task force on community and strategic alliances can be. The partnerships these discussions produce will go a long way toward putting in place the process, as that will leverage the institution's influence and reputation. Our previous discussions of alumni relations and athletics make the same case for their importance in finding students, raising money, and building reputation.

Vertical Task Forces

Vertical task forces are formed to more closely examine each program area. Each school and college should have one, and beyond that it is an institution-specific judgment about whether or not to have one for specific academic or co-curricular programs. These groups primarily perform SWOT analyses. They examine each program's strengths, weaknesses, opportunities, and threats.

STAFFING THE PROJECT

Part of what makes the participatory model work is the way volunteers combined with staff work together for a year or more. The volunteer project chair should be a very high profile graduate of the institution, someone with name recognition and a track record of high achievement. The power of this person's stature will give the whole project prestige, credibility, and visibility. The press coverage you get will largely be determined by the chair, and many other high-profile people will serve only when invited by a person of high regard. This person will be responsible for participating in preplanning discussions, helping recruit chairs for the task forces, signing the letter of invitation to all participants, presiding over the kickoff and final report meetings, and being a part of the whole process of analyzing the results. This volunteer chair will work directly with the staff executive director.

The staff executive director must be a ranking official of the institution assigned by the president to do this job. He or she must have at hand the staff resources to support the work and be able to delegate the other work of the office to someone else for this extended period of time. The staff executive director must have enough credibility to make faculty, staff, and others perceive the project as likely to produce positive change. This person may also appoint someone else to handle the logistics of the meetings.

Each task force should include both a volunteer chair and a staff facilitator. Volunteer chairs should be selected because of their stature and expertise in a field related to the task force topic. Each facilitator should also have a background related to the task force topic and access to clerical support. Facilitators can be either faculty or staff so long as they can arrange for the backup help that they will need to prepare for meetings.

THE MEETINGS

All 500 or so participants should be invited to a kickoff meeting where objectives are stated, the mission and vision of the institution reviewed, and a situation analysis of trends and issues presented. This should be a motivational meeting where the volunteer chair and the president preside. The first task force meetings should follow very soon, maybe even that day. One successful format is to have the kickoff at lunch followed immediately by two- to three-hour task force meetings.

After the kickoff the task forces set their own agendas and meeting times and places. They should meet at least five or six times over the course of nine months to a year, but they can meet as often as they want. Their charge is simply to produce a list of suggestions, but those suggestions should be the result of a lot of conversation and careful consideration.

Facilitators go through a training session to learn how to anticipate problems and suggest solutions. They gather the support materials they want to have on hand and analyze the individuals in their group. The facilitators then meet regularly with the executive director in groups and individually throughout the project to make progress reports and solve problems. Problem participants are dealt with individually outside of the meetings.

A project Web site is established so that all task force members can track the progress of all of the task forces. An abbreviated report of preliminary suggestions and comments is posted after each task force meeting. This Web site can be either password-protected or open to the public, but it is an important ingredient in making the whole project work. It is not uncommon for one task force to get into another task force's area of concern. By going to the Web site, a task force can quickly determine what the others are talking about.

The final report meeting is really a celebration of achievement. A summary of task force suggestions is delivered, and the project chairman and institution's president give a preview of how all of this work will be reviewed for implementation.

DETERMINING IMPLEMENTATION

The executive director should put together a group of colleagues to review the suggestions and determine which can be done for no money, which should be considered in the normal budgeting process, and which will require new money.

The major advisory and governing groups of the institution then review this analysis and rate the suggestions. These groups include

- President's cabinet
- Academic deans
- Middle managers group (if one exists)
- Faculty senate or leadership
- Staff senate or leadership
- Alumni board
- Board of trustees
- Advisory boards of specific programs

After full discussion about priorities, the decisions about what will or will not be done are made within the normal management structures of the institution. But because the planning process has been so participatory, there is now a predisposition within all of these groups to make exciting things happen. At the end of all the discussions, however, it will be up to the president's cabinet to translate these suggestions into a blueprint for action and to the board of trustees to find the new money for the bold new initiatives.

In this way the planning project becomes a staging mechanism for a comprehensive fundraising campaign. Because the trustees participated in the planning, they already know what's coming. And because most of the donors that will be needed to make a campaign successful participated in the project as well, they know what's coming and already feel ownership in the outcome.

FOLLOW-UP

Anticipated early outcomes of a participatory strategic planning project might very well include

- A clearer vision for the future
- A clearer set of priorities
- A sense that everyone is more on the same page about what makes the institution distinctive
- Direct lines of communication with those most likely to help shape the future
- Bonding to the institution and to each other
- A list of many improvements that can be made at low or no cost
- A list of the bold initiatives that will really make a difference

Of course, not all the suggestions will be implemented, but many of them will be. The dynamic of the process is such that the participants will feel pride in being part of the future of a grand institution, and they will feel connected for the long term.

The institution should take specific steps to make participants permanent alumni of the project. Send them regular progress reports, and treat them as insiders by inviting them to special events. They should receive all of the special news releases, publications, and perks that you offer your stakeholders. If you have a stakeholders program (as described earlier), the planning project participants should become a special group within it. Occasionally, you might invite them back to an update luncheon and a reunion with other participants.

When all is said and done, participatory strategic planning is the ultimate in integrated marketing. It is very effective and well worth all the time and effort.

CHAPTER EIGHTEEN

The Critical Role of Leadership

Integrated marketing doesn't happen without leadership. All the materials in the world, no matter how well-produced or well-organized, will not generate any more than a short-lived ripple unless the right people saying the right thing to the right people at the right time lead the whole process. There is something about enterprises and people that absolutely requires articulate leaders with vision standing out front.

Leadership is needed at all levels, beginning with the CEO. The personification of a set of ideas that offer hope for greater shared achievement is at the foundation of institutional marketing. People have to believe it can happen, and history makes it clear that groups and teams develop that belief only when they place their trust in a person who, they believe, understands how the world is changing.

But for marketing to be effective, leadership must happen in more places than at the top. Effective marketing requires a champion, a person who understands change in that field and can challenge the whole institution to learn more about how it applies to them. Writers need to lead other writers with new and creative ideas. Designers must challenge other designers with new visions. Electronic media people need to step out and lead others through the maze of a changing Internet and new digital technology. Indeed, for educational institutions to meet the challenge of a rapidly changing world, we need to seriously challenge our best thinkers to step out and lead.

This changing world of the 21st century presents unique challenges. There are whole new sets of problems to face, from new technology that is changing both systems and the way people think and function to a new economy that is virtually changing everything. Leaders at all levels are being challenged as never before.

New concerns about terrorism and personal safety, career opportunities and whole industries coming and going, and new demands for quality and service from intelligent consumers all demand a new level of leadership sophistication. Institutional leaders will have to not only understand academic trends and raise money, but in the future they will have to be more involved with finding students and building reputation. These 21st-century demands will require a new breed of leadership for education, and we will have to figure out where they will come from and how we will inspire them to satisfy the demands.

CONFRONTING CHANGE AND NEW TECHNOLOGY

The speed of change is staggering. We keeping looking ahead, but the changes are coming so fast it's almost impossible to see them. We study the past and learn those lessons, but change is happening so fast that there is almost no sense of the present. Leaders today have to jump into the technology and swim with the flow. It takes a person who can absorb and articulate what they are absorbing at the same time. In that sense leaders must become journalists of the highest order.

This highly charged environment requires fast decision making and a global perspective. The economy is international. News is international. Technology is international. It has made the world smaller and put us more in touch. But instead of erasing our differences, it has magnified them. Instead of producing understanding, it has increased fear and hostility—at least for the short term.

Furthermore, this digital world is producing new ways of thinking. A whole new generation will think differently about a lot of things. About work. About life beyond work. About spiritual matters. For this generation, it all will have to make sense as a part of a larger whole. Gone will be the days when one works to make money and separates that from life's real satisfactions. Work will have to be rewarding, have personal meaning. Work will have to acknowledge and accommodate a larger life beyond it. And leaders will have to understand how to make those accommodations without compromising the success of the organization. They will have to inspire and support high professional achievement within a context of having fun and supporting strong personal and family life.

CHARACTERISTICS OF LEADERS

Hears an Inner Voice

Somewhere in their lives, great leaders hear an inner voice. Many say it resembles a calling. When they hear it and respond, they begin to look almost driven. They will try to achieve no matter what. A task that needs to be done has connected with a matter of personal interest and concern. Soon they feel an emotion, a passion develops, and a leader with a cause is born.

Some talk about a "leadership moment." Something happens of some urgency. A person is in a difficult situation. And for reasons always difficult to completely explain, the person steps up to the challenge. "I was there and I decided to do it."

This is quite different from assuming the position of CEO or head of marketing. These positions require planning and managing but have nothing to do with whether or not the person will lead. A position is ascribed, but leadership must be acknowledged by followers and therefore must be earned. The moment occurs, but leadership is in place only after acknowledgment and recognition comes from the behaviors and rhetoric of followers. In other words, leadership has a kind of transcendent quality about it wherein followers can almost see that this person is driven by an inner voice.

Along with this voice must come an ability to see what is possible but also know what is desirable. This distinction is important because followers have to buy into the cause; to inspire them leaders have to articulate the link between possibility and desirability. And leaders generally can inspire because, in this link, they have also developed a sense that they are on to something unique. At the very least they see and feel excitement about a new spin.

Is Ambitious, But…

Effective leaders are generally ambitious people, but what differentiates them is that they are not also self-centered. They want to achieve but they also want to take others with them. They do their homework. They are always prepared, and preparation leads to a clarity of purpose. It is easy to see where they are going because their homework produces clarity of thinking and speaking.

Has Remarkable Persistence

Leaders never quit. They suffer setbacks. They can be momentarily derailed by circumstances. But they are never totally stopped. They automatically look for the way around a roadblock. They develop a mental habit of looking for alternatives. They almost always have a Plan B in mind if Plan A gets bogged down. Reaching a goal is a mental exercise that involves variations on the theme, not just playing a rigidly written score.

Persistence is not difficult for the leader because no other approach makes sense. If you quit, then what? This leads nowhere. There is no purpose in it, no place to go from there, especially when it seems so obvious that if you keep looking for the right path and keep going you will eventually get out of the woods. This is how leaders think differently from others.

Deals Positively with Failure

The logic about failure is the same as the logic about quitting. Failure is a natural part of learning on the way to success. The scientist runs an experiment, fails, makes changes, and then runs it again. Scientists expect to have countless failures before an experiment succeeds. Leaders who hear an inner voice see their work in the same way. Failure is expected. Failure is merely a learning opportunity. Not everyone can see it like this, but real leaders do.

Leaders therefore take risks—calculated risks. They are cautious about betting the whole ranch, but they take risks every day. But when their homework is done, they realize that achievements worth attaining involve a high measure of risk. If that were not the case, someone would have done it before. And if you fail, there is tomorrow.

Connects with People

The best leaders do not necessarily seem invincible. Many convey an appealing vulnerability. They stand strong, keep moving forward, but at the same time are approachable. Even from a distance they seem to be real people. They look like they could get hurt, but they rarely actually do. They are always able to flinch and keep going. It is a quality that makes large numbers of people feel almost a personal connection with them.

The most effective leaders collaborate with other people. They often perform best with two to three other talented people around them, and yet they stay visible and responsive to the larger group. Seeing leaders function comfortably in larger settings reinforces the impression that they really care about building meaningful relationships with colleagues.

Sees the Big Picture

Some minds can instinctively see the larger picture. They can see all the parts of the goal and put the entire challenge into perspective for others focused on only their part. They can look at a problem, see five or six solutions, and then explain them to the others. Not that they always know what to do right away. They do not. As mentioned before, they do their homework. They know how to work the data. But after the research is done, the difference is the way their mind works. They are able to picture all the parts of the goal or problem and then put these parts into real-world perspective.

Seeks Partnerships

In spite of the truism that it is lonely at the top, the best leaders avoid that loneliness as much as possible. Indeed, there are moments when the responsibility produces that feeling, but the most effective leaders are always cultivating and using collaborators, just as they seek formal partnerships for projects and new ventures wherever appropriate. It is important for leaders to have sounding boards and to have people they trust to turn to in difficult circumstances. There are moments when only one person can make a given decision, but the interaction that precedes that decision establishes an environment rich with ideas that the best leaders really need. Cultivating the right partners is a real talent of leadership.

Is Inspired by Creative People

The best leaders love other creative people, especially those who are creative in areas different from their own. Staying on top always involves searching for new ideas. Sometimes it's a new way to do an old project or a new way to say the same thing. For developing a brand name and building reputation, creativity is the real challenge. How do you stay on-message and establish a design consistency while you maintain vitality and look innovative? This is the most difficult kind of creativity.

Many leaders will surround themselves only with people they regard as creative. In education this would mean top officials in student affairs, finance and business, plant maintenance, academics, and fund raising as well as marketing and communication. Creativity on the president's cabinet means having people who can think outside the box while they keep their eye on the ball. And unlocking innovation everywhere should be an underlying theme of the entire administration. This makes for an energizing atmosphere and an overall positive climate.

This may sound contradictory but tolerance for ambiguity is one of a leader's most important qualities.

Has Tolerance for Ambiguity

This may sound contradictory but tolerance for ambiguity is one of a leader's most important qualities. People who feel they have to control every detail often make very poor leaders. Because their nature precludes them from seeing the big picture, they cannot inspire and excite others. As they get bogged down in details and become frustrated with those around them, eventually the climate turns negative.

The person who stays focused on the goal and keeps articulating the most important strategies for reaching it will be the better leader. And while this person must communicate concern about details and expectations, he or she must be able to function well without getting consumed by them. You can't control everything, and the leaders who sleep at night are those who can leave much of the operation to others.

Is on a Mission

When someone appears to be on a mission—especially if you share the same concerns—he or she becomes attractive to you. Leaders on a mission attract followers, and those followers make strong commitments. Making a goal a mission also involves appealing to values. A leader who hears an inner voice associated with a concern for basic human values can therefore be said to be on a mission. It becomes the goal of an effective leader to get everyone in the organization on a mission. As described previously, this can be a theme of internal marketing and communication.

Has a Passion for the Business

Passion for the business is another characteristic of the most effective leaders. They love computers, or they love clothes, or they love cars, or they love music, or they love education. They just love the business they are in.

In education they are consumed with the beauty of the whole enterprise. They love teaching and teachers. The act of discovery is an exulting emotional experience. Artistic creation of all kinds is an absolute wonder. The cutting edge of change in education is the most exciting possible place to be. They cannot contain their love of their business, and they are always telling everybody about it. Leaders at all levels of the organization must have this passion for their professional area of expertise and for the business of education.

Creates a Learning Organization

Love of the business produces a desire to learn all there is to know about it. For the best leaders, this goes beyond their personal commitment to professional development. They become totally committed to the idea that the most successful organization will know more about the business than the competition, and that constant learning is important for everyone.

They will invest in and expand training and development. They will support real professional development and question travel to conferences that offer little of it. They will urge people to read in their field and to set personal goals to become leaders in their profession. They will talk about being on top, staying there, and what it takes to do it. And they will host meetings and forums that ask people to teach each other what they are learning. And when new ideas come forth, the leader will reward them handsomely.

Stays Positive, But...

A leader doesn't seem focused on problem solving or preoccupied with negative evaluation. His or her focus is not on investigating what is going wrong or uncovering what staff is doing wrong. Rather the leader is on a search for what works, for positive and inspirational role models. Leaders are affirming.

The key is to ask people, "What excites you?" When the leader can get people to focus on creating the conditions where everything works well, the place will move forward. An atmosphere of "I know you are doing something wrong" is counterproductive to the leader's goals.

When a person becomes a known problem or a program is not working, without dwelling on the negative the leader acts swiftly to fix it. If it means firing someone or ending a project, it is done with consideration for the human consequences, but it is done quickly so that the communication can again become positive just as quickly.

Has a Feel for Process

An orientation for organizational process is of increasing importance in this highly charged time of change. In the digital world described earlier, it is more important than ever to promote participatory planning and problem solving. This entire book has been about participatory marketing and participatory strategic planning. At a time when the entire institution needs to be mobilized, this style of leading and managing is the most effective.

This means that in addition to presenting information at meetings, the leader encourages and facilitates dialogue. He or she knows and encourages the creative potential of teams. Listening is an institutional value, and making human connection a shared goal. The effective leader asks every manager to take the time for open dialogue and to set up group processes to address issues. To the autocrat it seems a waste of time, but in the long run it actually saves time because better decisions are made and the bonding that occurs is a real investment in the future.

Because the strong leader therefore builds organizations by building community, there is a strong interest in internal marketing and communication. There is a strong interest in each and every employee. A major effort is made to make employee concerns very important to others. Publications report the human-interest side of the lives of employees. Employees are recognized for every level of achievement. Their lives and anniversaries are celebrated. All of this is critical because it is this community building that in the end enables organizational success.

Works the Politics

Even top leaders need to pay attention to organizational politics. There are trustees and donors for CEOs to be concerned about. Cabinet members compete with each other for resources and influence. Indeed, there are political concerns at every level of the organizations. And while the presence of politics might be unappealing, it is a fact of organizational life.

Effective leaders at all levels take politics in stride. The basic questions are, "What do I need help to do? Who do I need help from?" The answers define who you need to cultivate relationships with and pay attention to. Without compromising principles, it is very possible to ask, "Where can I help others?" The effective leader will take the time and initiative to offer to help others achieve their goals wherever possible. They will consider this an investment in support for their projects and will not resent any part of the process. The effective leader does not strive to win at any cost.

Can Manage Conflict

When conflict occurs, effective leaders know how to manage it. First of all, it happens often enough that it is very important to learn that conflicts are natural and need not produce excessive anger. Taking the attitude that conflict is normal helps the leader take the situation in stride.

Managing conflict usually involves taking the time to actively listen to all points of view, and then set up a decision or review process that all parties can see as fair. Both parties may not be happy, but in most cases the real reason for emotion in the conflict—the feeling that "No one listens to me around here"—disappears. Leaders take the time to listen, even when it takes time they don't have.

Defines Quality

Leaders are obsessed with quality, which is especially important in education. The most effective leaders define quality in terms of outcomes and challenge people in the organization to accept responsibility for producing it. Vision, energy, and enthusiasm are contagious, and they are often symptomized by a preoccupation with producing the best. This focus on outcomes is especially important for education in the 21st century. Delivering real quality is what will save institutions in the future; defining it and making sure it happens will be the primary work of its leaders.

Loves Marketing

Stemming from their love of the business, most leaders love marketing. They love thinking in terms of product, price, place, and promotion, and they love telling the stories that differentiate their products. It is a way of thinking that comes naturally to them.

This has not always been the case in education, but it will have to be more so in the future. For institutions to become and remain competitive in this changing marketplace, leaders will have to be engaged in the whole process. Presidents especially will have to be out front with fund raising, student recruiting, and reputation building. This, of course, goes hand-in-hand with their love of the business.

COMMUNICATION BEHAVIORS OF LEADERS

For leaders to be effective, all of these qualities I have been discussing have to be exhibited in communication behaviors. This is especially true if the marketing and communication program is to succeed. Leaders at all levels, but most especially the president, will have to reinforce the central messages, communicate the competitive advantage, and build relationships with stakeholders and opinion leaders in the major market segments. The institutional leaders must lead the marketing program; otherwise it will not be as effective as it should be. Here are some essential communication behaviors:

- *Possesses presence and charisma.* "Charisma" does not mean physical attractiveness and personal slickness. Rather it is a kind of attraction created when self-confident people stand out front and convince others that there is a fundamental excitement and benefit in working together to achieve a goal.
- *Is articulate and concise.* In a world of sound bites, leaders must be articulate and concise when they explain complex ideas. They must repeat themselves more than they expect, and they should be brief more often than not.
- *Expresses vision and goals.* Expressing visions and goals over and over again is the job of leadership. Creative leaders find new and refreshing ways of doing so.
- *Affirms values.* Corporate culture is an element of community that is essential to teamwork and success. Developing it is a major job of leadership, and communicating it constantly is critical.
- *Offers encouragement.* "You can do it" is what a coach says, and much of leadership is coaching. Talented people need encouraging coaches just as talented athletes do.
- *Takes time to explain.* This is a simple but essential communication behavior. There are so many assumptions in most organizations: "I know it, so I assumed you knew it too." People like to receive simple explanations of goals, policies, benefits, responses to crises, and anything else that directly affects them. And they want to get that explanation directly from the appropriate leader, not in a publication or memo.

People like to receive simple explanations of goals, policies, benefits, responses to crises, and anything else that directly affects them. And they want to get that explanation directly from the appropriate leader, not in a publication or memo.

- *Serves as a symbol.* Logos, buildings, and icons all become symbols of what an organization stands for. Leaders do too. When they stand out front, they visually personify the institution, its central message, and special niche in the world. It is an important part of the branding process for leaders to do this often.
- *Represents the group.* It is important that followers feel that their leaders represent their best interests at other levels of the organization and in the world, even when there may be disagreements on specific issues. This can be conveyed in the way leaders communicate and in what they choose to talk about.
- *Demonstrates a capacity for renewal.* Every leader and every organization over time reach plateaus. People feel forward movement has stalled, internal communication problems become the focus for criticism, and there is a general feeling that the place is being left behind by the competition. At this time, leaders need to either launch a renewal or be replaced. This capacity for renewal is a feature of the best leaders, which is how they manage to remain in the role for so long. And the best leaders know when it's time to make it a theme of their communication.

Materials and campaigns cannot do the marketing communications job alone. Leaders at all levels need to be out front articulating the vision and clarifying the competitive advantage. Only then can the rest of marketing communications do the job of supporting the initiative.

Leadership in the 21st century, no matter the level of the organization, faces some very important challenges. From a technology revolution to a new economy to a more competitive student-recruitment market to a more sophisticated consumer to a generation that thinks differently about life itself, the challenges of the leaders of education will be huge.

Where will these leaders come from? They will need to be academic visionaries who understand how marketing adapts to the academy, as well as to possess all of the other qualities I have described. Finding and developing them will be a real challenge.

CHAPTER NINETEEN

Evaluating the Results

One of the biggest challenges professionals in marketing and communication face is evaluating the results of their work. Certainly you could argue that if you are recruiting good students, raising money, and reducing complaints about visibility, you are getting the job done. Of course, there is some truth to that.

But success does not tell you what initiatives are working best and how to fine tune the marketing mix to make it all work better. The world is changing very rapidly; success today doesn't ensure success tomorrow. Integrated marketing is a way to set up a self-monitoring and ongoing process. Its built-in feedback provides the information you need to make changes as you go.

EVALUATION BUILT INTO THE PROCESS

When this kind of participatory process is functioning, participants understand what is working and what is not working. It is still difficult to prove with hard data, but being in the process—one day developing the materials, the next day as part of the communication process, and a day later day experiencing the responses—you feel confident about how things are going. And the longer you are in the process and the more experience you get, the more credible your judgments are likely to be.

This feeling of confidence extends to all those involved in integrated marketing, including those active in task force work. The more key people who are involved, the fewer key people you will have to prove results to. This is not a gimmick, but rather an expansion of the number of people who will experience what professionals have been experiencing all along—trust in what they are learning over time.

Ask only what you need to know and no more. You should be finding out how people have heard about you and what they think about you ...

RESEARCH AS EVALUATION

Considering all the surveys and focus groups you should conduct to determine the needs of your target market, it is difficult to imagine adding a whole array of other evaluation activities to your workload. There will not be time to do the marketing. But you should also consider your basic research work as evaluation. Don't make research instruments too long. Ask only what you need to know and no more. You should be finding out how people have heard about you and what they think about you as a part of other surveys and focus groups you do.

Awareness, Attitude, and Knowledge Surveys

These studies assess overall awareness of the institution, what people think about it, and how much they know about its programs. Three simple questions can elicit useful evaluation information: How did you first hear about us? Which communications were the most effective? Why?

Communications Audits

Initial communications audits are usually conducted internally by members of the marketing task force. As admissions and advancement people travel about, they should occasionally ask key stakeholders to critique key pieces of the communication mix. Flattered to be asked, stakeholders almost always eagerly respond. In fact, when getting in to see someone might be difficult, a request for ideas about communicating the institution may serve as a reason to make a call.

Opinion Leaders and Stakeholders

In addition to asking these people to audit materials during personal calls, you can from time to time send simple evaluation forms to your stakeholder list. Previously, I argued that integrated marketing favors communicating directly with the stakeholders in target markets, and that you should have a separate program for sending them all kinds of "inside" information. A major part of that program should include asking them what they think.

Media Gatekeepers

Sending simple postcard evaluation forms to editors and key writers can be helpful. Do they notice the information you send? Is it in a form they can use? Of course, your clips will tell another part of the story. Media people usually respond well to these postcards because few communications professionals bother to ask them what they think. This also serves a way to stand out with them and strengthen that all-important relationship. But even the clips, evidence of success in media placement, do not tell you who saw those stories and what they got from them.

Customer Satisfaction

Customer satisfaction surveys are designed to find out about what you can do to improve attrition rates. Implied are the questions: Did we deliver what we promised? How effective is our communication? Make sure through the wording of the questions that they evaluate your marketing as well as your programs.

Pricing Elasticity

Even pricing elasticity studies can provide some evaluation information. For example, you may ask, Other than lowering our price, what can we do to improve recruiting? Where were we effective? Usually these studies ask where students who did not attend because of price enrolled. This will give you an impression of how your reputation-building efforts are developing.

Freshman Focus Groups

It is particularly useful to talk to second-semester freshmen because they remember how they were recruited and can make judgments about what they found. This can be some of the most useful evaluation information you can gather. You may want them to audit materials as well as to make suggestions about how to improve them. Some of their suggestions will be naïve, but others may be brilliant. Either way, you get a very good impression of what does and does not impress them.

Current Parent Surveys

Whether by mail or telephone the questions to ask include, From your perspective, is your student getting what we promised? How do you rate our communication with you so far? What do you need? Many schools have parent's councils or groups of parent leaders. Their meetings are good times to conduct focus groups on these questions. It is a great way to continue to build relationships, and if they are impressed with their student's experience, current parents can be very helpful. They will give you money on top of their tuition if they have the means, and they are certainly among your very best word-of-mouth recruiters.

Prospect Surveys

Now often done by e-mail, prospect surveys elicit feedback about your communications while you are still in the process of communicating. This is about as efficient as you can get. Do not be afraid to ask them. They will tell you and respect you for it. How did you first hear about us? How do you rate what you have received so far? What do you want to get now?

Prospect Parent Surveys

These are more difficult to do, but you can do them by mail or telephone. Are you aware of what your students have received? How do you rate it? Are you getting what you need? If not, what do you want? Sometimes marketers choose to talk to prospect parents in focus groups during campus visits or during campus visit events. These groups can be very helpful.

School Counselors

The best time to reach these people is during your recruiter's visit to their schools. Most recruiters tell them only about their schools. How many ask the counselors what they think? Almost always they will take the time to answer a few questions. How effective are our materials? How can we improve them? How do we compare to others? This last question is the most important for counselors because they will provide your most useful feedback.

Magazine Surveys

Usually these surveys evaluate only the magazine but they can be very useful to editors. Some institutional magazines are little read at all, and some are rated among the most enjoyed communications received. Obviously, knowing your rating is critical. An inserted postcard can help you assess overall attitude and gain a sense of priority for the kinds of stories and information readers prefer.

Internal Media Readers Surveys

Simple postcard surveys are helpful. As with magazines, you can assess overall value to the reader and determine what story topics and types of information they prefer. It is also possible to ask, In what other ways would you like to receive information? Internal e-mail newsletters and more direct communication from managers are most often requested.

Community Focus Groups

Conducting focus groups throughout the community can be a very effective communication and evaluation tool. Within each target market, form several small groups. Stick to basic questions. How do you rate the university on a scale of one to 10? How do you rate our communication with you? What are your needs? How can we improve?

GROUP DYNAMICS

Contact with each group provides an opportunity to describe the marketing task force, the niche you fill in education, your competitive advantage, and your basic goals—especially those for building stronger community partnerships. When you do this at the same time that you ask for feedback, you have created the strongest possible relationship-building formula. These groups can be so successful that you might make them an ongoing part of your program.

These groups can be especially helpful in building relationships with minority communities for eventually improving diversity on campus. First you need to find out why minorities do not attend your institution. Then you need to build trust with their community leaders. And then you need to be perceived as involved with addressing their concerns. A combination of communications and evaluation through focus groups can go a long way toward realizing greater diversity.

For the bold marketer, these groups can lead to forums with larger community organizations. Instead of taking speakers to civic groups and professional associations, you can offer a facilitated discussion. These too are opportunities to communicate where you are headed while you find out what people think. Of course, the public nature of these meetings may make you feel a little insecure about what might happen. Usually the outcome is more positive than negative. You can lessen the sting of negative criticism by what you say up front, and you will automatically sound impressive when you talk about the new initiatives underway at your institution. And, of course, you are demonstrating the institution's openness to new ideas by just being there. The whole context of this kind of meeting communicates an image of a serious, self-confident institution on the move that will become a more and more important asset to the community in the years ahead.

In marketing, research and program evaluation go hand-in-hand. Finding out about the needs of target markets are also opportunities for seeking feedback on how you are doing. In the final analysis, integrated marketing is a process that seeks to build feedback and evaluation into the ongoing process of communication. Those who are involved in the process will be able to adjust the program to market and evaluate information on a day-to-day basis.

CHAPTER TWENTY

A Final Word:
Managing Change in the Academy

Managing change is what this book has really been about. And it has also tried to demonstrate that marketing and communication—given the nature of what is going on in the world—has to be a major part of the picture. New technology, a new economy, and intense competition have already established a new playing field. The leaders of educational enterprises worldwide will have to change in light of those market realities.

Change is painful, especially for institutions with long historical traditions. Educational institutions exist not to give people what they want but rather to give them what they will need. The critics of marketing ask, What good could come of turning the academy over to marketers? Won't giving students what they say they want turn us into a retail store?

When adapted to the academy, marketing does nothing of the sort. Rather, it uses perceived needs only as a point of departure. From that point on, by considering programs, pricing, program delivery, and communication all at the same time, it first demands true quality and then insists on delivering what it promises.

Marketing provides information that helps program planners make sure they are meeting the needs of a changing society, not just satisfying the needs of 18-year-olds.

The only threat of marketing is that it may show some institutions that they are not as good as they think they are. Marketing provides information that helps program planners make sure they are meeting the needs of a changing society, not just satisfying the needs of 18-year-olds. Indeed, the aim of marketing is high: to make the place the best it can be at doing what it does.

By clarifying its competitive advantage, an institution has the opportunity to become the best of its kind rather than an also-ran on a long list of comparable institutions. Marketing is reality therapy. It makes you find out what you do well and stop kidding yourself about what you don't do well. It liberates you from thinking you are second or third tier, and it shows you how to manage yourself to a new and credible level of distinction.

Marketing is indeed a way of thinking, not commercializing, and as such it is compatible in every way with the pursuits of intellectuals. It bases its recommendations on research, and it insists on applying reason to the strategies and tactics it recommends. It is compatible with the academy in every way.

Integrated marketing is collegial in that it sets up processes that involve all segments of the organization, faculty, staff, and students. Everyone with talent is able to use it, and everyone with ideas gets heard. Since the process is ongoing, there is never a moment when someone can feel that his or her input arrived too late to count.

The student services that marketing calls for are services that institutions know they need to upgrade anyway. But once housing and food service and recreational facilities are in place, marketing research makes it clear that it is the experience of these things that matters most. Again, the demand marketing makes is for quality. The demand is that a service promised becomes a service delivered, and that professionals and support staff in every corner of the campus take pride in the quality of what they do.

With all of the issues on the horizon that the academy has to face, we have made a case here for the development of leaders who understand the complex new landscape and can effectively manage change. The bottom line is that it will take people who understand marketing not as sales, but as a participatory planning activity that makes the institution susceptible to social change. It will require rethinking core education requirements, the role and potential threat of for-profit education, actual uses and costs of technology, what it really means to be global, the relationship of distance education to resident-based education, and how all of this is to be communicated. It will require a new breed of leadership.

In no way should any of this compromise the standards of academia. Its leaders will still need to be firmly grounded in teaching and research. They will still need to have the deepest respect of the faculty and staff. But now more than ever they also will have to orchestrate a process that gets everyone on the same page and pulling in the same direction.

This leadership will have to be at all levels of the organization and within every unit, academic and support. Everyone will have to be well versed in all of what it will take to compete for students, money, and reputation. And it will take them all working as a team to be successful.

Ten Steps to Integrated Marketing

Objective: To adapt the latest thinking about integrated and relationship marketing to the academy in order to enhance competitiveness and organizational effectiveness, especially as they relate to visibility, admissions, fund raising, alumni relations, curriculum planning, student programs planning, and overall morale.

ESSENTIAL FACTORS

1. Set up an internal education *process* to establish marketing as *a way of thinking* throughout the organization, concentrating on *opinion leaders*.
2. Clarify *mission* and *vision* and translate them into a *competitive advantage*-based message, and then get everyone *on the same page*.
3. Establish a strategic marketing task force as an activity of the CEO's *office,* and find a *champion* to manage it.
4. Identify *market segments* and the *opinion leaders* within them, including *internal* segments.
5. Do an *audit* of current marketing communication for *consistency* of *identity, message and intensity*, review the audit with the *market segments* in mind.

6. Establish ongoing *survey and focus group* research for *each market segment to assess awareness, attitude, knowledge,* and *price elasticity*.
7. Determine *priorities* and set goals, i.e. more applications and greater visibility.
8. Establish *action teams* for *market segment initiatives*, and then outline an *action blueprint*.
9. Focus on *branding* the institution and plan *visibility*, determining with whom and at what cost.
10. Build feedback *evaluation* into the total process as a part of research, planning, and team discussions.

Discussion Questions for a Marketing Task Force

UNDERSTANDING YOUR COMPETITIVE ENVIRONMENT

1. To what institution do we compare ours?
2. What institutions do we aspire to emulate?
3. With what institutions do we actually compete for students?
4. What are their competitive assets?
5. What is our competitive advantage?
6. What are the behavior characteristics of our prospective students, parents, donors, etc.?
7. How do we segment our marketplace?
8. What effectiveness issues do we face?
9. How do we define quality?

UNDERSTANDING YOUR MARKETING MIX

1. What are the actual products we provide?
2. How do we set our price?
3. How effective is the distribution of what we provide?
4. How effective is our communication (messages, materials, channels, feedback)?
5. What is the most effective way to segment our market?

THE POWER OF BRAND NAME

1. How does the concept of brand relate to academic institutions?
2. How do we go about building our brand?
3. What are the implications of building a brand name for our communications office?

THE ROLE OF ADVERTISING

1. When is advertising a waste of time for colleges and universities?
2. What kinds of advertising have we done?
3. When has it been effective?

THE ROLE OF RESEARCH

1. Why haven't colleges and universities done more market research?
2. What kinds of studies have we done?
3. What kinds are the most helpful?

BARRIERS TO MARKETING THE ACADEMY

1. What are the major roadblocks to marketing in our institution?
2. How can we best remove them?
3. What pegs or circumstances can we use as reasons to launch a program?

ORGANIZING YOUR ASSAULT

1. What units in our institution now do marketing?
2. How could we best get them to integrate their efforts?
3. How might we organize a task force?
4. How might we reorganize the administration?
5. What is the role of institutional leadership?
6. Who can be effective as the marketing champion?

DEVELOPING A PLAN

1. What planning format will work best for us?
2. Do we have mission and vision statements? How can we clarify them?
3. What are our main concerns/goals?
4. What major initiatives will best address them?
5. How can we get everyone on the same page?

MARKETING INSIDE

1. How can we get everyone inside to know the mission and share the vision?
2. How can we improve performance reward and recognition?
3. How can we differentiate between internal communications and internal marketing?
4. How can we mobilize our talent and resources to help tell our story?
5. What do we know about our customer satisfaction?
6. How can we improve our customer service?

HOW MARKETING CHANGES OPERATIONS

1. How should marketing change our admissions office?
2. How can we organize the most effective office of communications?
3. What are the implications of marketing for alumni and donor relations? Athletics? The bookstore? Etc.?

OVERALL INSTITUTIONAL STRATEGIC PLANNING

1. How should marketing change overall institutional planning?
2. Is it appropriate for trustees to get involved in marketing?

A 14-Step Marketing Plan

1. State institutional mission.
2. State institutional vision.
3. State institutional values.
4. List institutional goals for current year.
5. State marketing division mission.
6. State marketing division vision.
7. State marketing division values.
8. List marketing goals for current year.
9. List specific initiatives to reach each goal.
10. List themes and write central message that describe competitive advantage.
11. List target market segments.
12. List the appropriate initiatives (selected from number 9) under each market segment. Make certain they reinforce the central themes.
13. Distribute the same initiatives under each appropriate communications administrative unit and/or staff member for implementation.
14. Ask each communications unit to develop a three-month action schedule with completion times and to update it frequently.

The Texas Christian University Marketing and Communication Division

Texas Christian University is a major teaching and research university with the personalized atmosphere of a smaller college. It is a global-minded university that maintains the traditions of a private college. The marketing and communication division develops strategic plans and initiatives to build the university's reputation, recruit students, and find resources. It seeks to communicate a better understanding of TCU's strengths, character, mission, and goals. It analyzes audiences, designs messages, and selects media to support these objectives. The division operates much as an internal public relations and advertising agency, utilizing a creative team approach to marketing and communication problem-solving.

The *vice chancellor for marketing and communication* oversees the development of strategic marketing and communication plans and activities for individual programs, as well as for the university as a whole. He or she is also responsible for overseeing the development of communications support and materials for student recruiting and fund raising, handling communications related to sensitive issues and crises, coordinating various community and city-related projects, working with the chancellor's staff on communications-related matters, and handling the university's relations with the state legislature. He or she has oversight of the offices of Communications, Publications, Editorial Services, Special Projects, Web Management, Development Communications, and of the Faculty Center.

MARKETING

Day-to-day marketing activities take place in departments in various divisions of the university. These include: undergraduate admissions, graduate admissions, communications, media relations, government relations, special events, extended education, athletics, advancement, student affairs programs, the bookstore, international programs, and more. However, the institution's overall marketing priorities are set and major initiatives are coordinated through three levels of advisory and implementation groups. These advisory and coordination groups report directly to the Office of the Chancellor and are managed by the vice chancellor for marketing and communication.

TCU Marketing Advisory Board (MAB)

The MAB has representation from all of the marketing-related departments in the university, the board of trustees, and other external volunteers. It meets three or four times per year to (1) identify marketing issues and (2) recommend effective responses. The MAB also helps communicate the university's marketing program to its constituents and works to get everyone on the same page with respect to institutional message and positioning.

TCU Marketing Management Committee

This committee translates the ideas of the advisory board into strategic implementation plans. Its members are marketing professionals from inside the university and include the chairs of specific marketing action groups. The committee (1) sets overall marketing planning priorities, (2) reviews and approves specific target marketing initiatives, and (3) oversees marketing research projects.

TCU Marketing Action Groups

The Marketing Management Committee creates specific action groups to implement priority strategic marketing initiatives. These groups are small and consist of experts in professional areas needed for activity implementation. The university currently has action groups in the areas of undergraduate student recruitment, visibility and reputation building, internal marketing, donor and alumni relations, and athletics.

- The *Admissions Action Group* (1) audits the marketing communications mix of materials and personal contacts each year and makes appropriate message, design, and timing adjustments; and (2) identifies special market segments which require special attention. Campaigns are currently being designed to recruit Hispanic and African-American students, to find and recruit more males, and to find and recruit more students from outside Texas, all to improve the overall balance of the campus community.
- The *Visibility Action Group* oversees the university's major initiatives in (1) institutional advertising, (2) public relations, and (3) strategic planning for promoting selected centers of excellence. This group determines which reputation-defining news stories will receive special attention and overall advertising priorities while it helps develop and promote critical special events. The visibility group helped write the strategic plan for the International Fine Arts Board of Visitors, developed the *Texas Monthly* advertising campaign, is designing a campaign to strengthen relationships between the university and the Hispanic and African-American communities, and more.
- The *Internal Action Group* is striving to (1) get everyone in the university to tell the TCU story, (2) strengthen core values and traditions, (3) develop a service orientation in the behavior of all TCU people, and (4) improve attendance at special and athletics events.

- The *Advancement Action Group* is working on ways integrated marketing practices can enhance the work of professional fund raisers and alumni programmers. It will (1) implement a post-campaign communication plan with broad-based initiatives to build support for fund-raising priorities, (2) identify new ways to involve the total university in strengthening relationships with donors, and (3) design a comprehensive plan to involve alumni families in a lifelong relationship with the whole university.
- The *Athletics Action Group* (1) oversees the setting of themes and overall initiatives of the athletics-marketing program, and (2) plans ways to use athletics to promote the total university.

COMMUNICATIONS

Ten administrative areas of activity report directly to the vice chancellor for marketing and communication, and they (1) support the work of the Marketing Advisory Board, Marketing Management Committee, and action groups; and (2) manage the day-to-day communications and information activities of the university.

Office of Communications

The director and staff of Communications (1) help units inside the university develop strategic communications and marketing plans, (2) handle all news-media relations, (3) are responsible for internal communications, (4) assist with various video production projects, and (5) research advertising opportunities.

- *Getting the word out.* Information about faculty, staff and student achievements, projects and events should be sent to this office. All information must be complete and specific: names, descriptions, times, locations, name and phone number of contact person, and deadline information. Priority must be given to items that support the university's central message and goals. This office will consider and carry out communications activities directly with key audiences, not just news media contacts.

• *Handling sensitive issues and crisis.* The Office of Communications will prepare a fact sheet for all issues relating to official university business that has public interest. The vice chancellor, with the help of the director of communications, will form a management committee when necessary, appoint spokespersons, and help them organize and prepare statements. The purpose is always to tell the truth and tell it quickly—and to be mindful of the public's need to know, the university's legitimate interests, other privacy considerations, and liability concerns.

• *Interviews with the press.* On sensitive matters related to official university business, it is requested that faculty and staff work directly with the director of communications and/or the vice chancellor. On matters related to other day-to-day stories, faculty and staff are urged to cooperate with the news media and to return their calls promptly. Some faculty and staff, due to the nature of their research or creative activity, will cultivate their own relationships. Any contact, however, should be coordinated with this office, so that the communications staff can maximize exposure and be fully aware of news media activities.

• *News and events online.* Recent news announcements, links to feature stories, an events calendar, and general TCU information can all be easily accessed on the TCU Web site (http://tcu.pressrelease.com). Current headlines appear on the news bar (www.tcu.edu), enabling the TCU community and any visitor to the TCU Web site to remain abreast of TCU-related news and events. The news site and headlines are updated weekly or more frequently as news occurs. This site also will be a primary source of news and information during a crisis or emergency.

• *Internal communications. TCU This Week* is the primary internal communications periodical. *TCU This Week* is distributed each Monday, and all news and information for it must be turned in to the internal communications editor by noon on the Monday of the week prior to publication. An additional publication, *Inside TCU*, reinforces the feeling of community between faculty and staff members with people-oriented features and profiles. Published five times annually, issues are mailed to faculty and staff members' homes the first week of the month of publication. The deadline for submitting news and calendar items is one month before the publication date. All items for internal publications should be submitted via e-mail (news@tcu.edu) or on paper via campus mail.

- *Biographical data.* Data cards and photos are maintained on faculty and high-profile staff. It is important to help keep these cards current since they are used when preparing communications materials and news stories.
- *Experts guide.* This office maintains lists of topics and TCU experts. They are sent to the news media as suggestions for quotes and interviews and to community organizations as possible speakers and programs. Often, faculty and staff are contacted directly. These activities promote TCU's visibility and are a desirable way to promote public awareness of TCU's community involvement.
- *Advertising.* TCU does a limited amount of institutional advertising, most of it placed in the community for visibility with targeted priority audiences. Some departments have advertising budgets and are urged to seek help here for developing messages and concepts.

Office of Editorial Services

The director and staff serve as the "university editor" and are responsible for writing, editing and/or reviewing for accuracy and style all official publications and periodicals.

- *The TCU Magazine.* The official TCU magazine is sent four times each year to alumni and other university constituents.
- *Official catalogues.* Some are updated every two years, others as needed.
- *Regional newsletters and calendars.* Special newsletters are currently prepared for the north Texas region and the Houston area.

Office of Publications

The director and staff handle the design and print production management for all official university publications.

- *Budgeting*. The ordering department must pay for the printing of any publication not specifically listed in the central communications budget. No charges are made, however, for design or management time. Cost estimates can be furnished for the purpose of departmental budgeting. No liabilities are assumed for cost overruns, which can happen in large-job printing.
- *Ordering*. Work-order forms must be filled out in full with deadline needs clearly indicated and agreed to by the director of publications. Please note that no job begins until all information is in hand, including final copy. This office handles more than 500 projects each year. Stationery, business cards, and mailing labels are ordered directly from TCU Printing Services.
- *Copywriting*. Final drafts can be submitted to the publications office as hard copy or on a computer disk in virtually any word-processing program (Macintosh or PC). Copywriting assistance is available from the editorial services office as their time permits.
- *Quality standards*. Publications designed for official off-campus distribution must conform to TCU Graphics Guidelines: They must be designed by publications-office-approved graphics professionals, typeset or printed by a computer printer with resolution higher than 300 DPI, and printed on appropriate paper stock. They must also utilize a consistent, high-quality printing process (not electrostatic).
- *Desktop publishing*. TCU guidelines urge that you avoid more than three type fonts on a piece, large solid or screened areas, type fonts smaller than nine points for laser output, elements that bleed off the page and cluttered designs. We suggest that you consult with the Office of Publications.

Office of Special Projects

The director of special projects handles all official university events and other special community relations marketing and communication projects.

- *Events*. Commencements, groundbreakings, dedications, convocations, special receptions, etc., are included. University schools, colleges, and departments may request planning assistance on a time-available basis.
- *Projects*. This office assists the vice chancellor with community activities, such as projects with neighborhood associations, special reports about community activities, etc.
- *The Faculty Center*. This office manages the day-to-day activities of the center, including the scheduling of events.

Admissions Marketing

The admissions marketing director reports both to the vice chancellor for marketing and communication and the dean of admissions. Responsibilities include (1) preparation, testing, and evaluation of all admissions marketing materials; (2) recruiting communication process planning and management; and (3) planning and implementation of special initiatives to meet specific goals.

Legislative Relations

The vice chancellor serves as the university's government-relations officer. This primarily involves working with Independent Colleges and Universities of Texas (ICUT) on state legislative relations and with the mayor and city staff on Fort Worth relationship-building projects. The university is not active in federal legislative relations, but it is represented by its grants administration office in matters related to research.

Crisis Communications and Issues Management

The vice chancellor and the director of communications work directly with the chancellor, other vice chancellors, and others on developing plans and strategies for managing crises and handling sensitive issues.

Web Management

The director of Web management oversees the development of TCU's presence on the Internet and in other new media.

Development Communications

The director of development communications develops the communications-support strategies, plans, tactics and materials for annual fund raising and comprehensive campaigns.

Selected Bibliography

Albrighton, Frank and Julia Thomas, Eds. *Managing External Relations.* Open University Press, 2001.

Beckwith, Harry. *The Invisible Touch: The Four Keys to Modern Marketing.* Warner Books, 2000.

Beckwith, Harry. *Selling the Invisible: A Field Guide to Modern Marketing.* Warner Books, 1997.

Berry, Leonard L. *On Great Service: A Framework for Action.* Free Press, 1995.

Buchanan, Peter McE., Ed. *Handbook of Institutional Advancement,* 3rd ed. Council for Advancement and Support of Education, 2000.

The CASE International Journal of Educational Advancement, October 2000.

D'Aprx, Roger. *Communicating for Productivity.* Harper & Row, 1982.

Deal, Terrence E. and Allan A. Kennedy. *Corporate Cultures: The Rite and Rituals of Corporate Life.* Addison-Wesley, 1982.

Depree, Max. *Leadership Is an Art.* Doubleday, 1989.

Dilenschneider, Robert L. *A Briefing for Leaders: Communication as the Ultimate Exercise of Power.* HarperCollins, 1992.

Drucker, Peter F. *Managing the Non-Profit Organization: Principles and Practice.* Harperbusiness, 1990.

Gralla, Preston. *How the Internet Works*. Que Macmillan Computer Publishing, 1999.

Hamilton, Seymour Charles. *A Communication Audit Handbook: Helping Organizations Communicate*. Longman Group UK, 1987.

Hampden-Turner, Charles. *Creating Corporate Culture*. Addison-Wesley, 1992.

Hoffman, Allan M., ed., John H. Schuh and Robert H. Fenske. *Violence on Campus: Defining the Problems, Strategies for Action*. Aspen Publishers, 1998.

Ind, Nicholas. *The Corporate Brand*. New York University Press, 1997.

Innis, Harold A. *The Bias of Communication*. University of Toronto Press, 1991.

Kotler, Phillip and Karen F.A. Fox. *Strategic Marketing for Educational Institutions*. Prentice-Hall, 1985.

Kotter, John P. *Leading Change*. Harvard Business School Press, 1996.

Lamb, Charles, et al. *Marketing & Technology*. South-Western Publishing, 1996.

Lauer, Larry D. *Communication Power: Energizing Your Nonprofit Organization*. Aspen Publishers, 1997.

Lerbinger, Otto. *Managing Corporate Crises: Strategies for Executives*. Barrington Press, 1986.

Luther, William M. *The Marketing Plan: How to Prepare and Implement It*. AMACOM, 1992.

McKenna, Regis. *Relationship Marketing: Successful Strategies for the Age of the Customer*. Addison-Wesley, 1991.

McLuhan, M. *Understanding Media: The Extensions of Man*. McGraw-Hill, 1966.

Nanus, Burt and Stephen M. Dobbs. *Leaders Who Make a Difference: Essential Strategies for Meeting the Nonprofit Challenge*. Jossey-Bass, 1999.

Pinsdorf, Marion K. *Communicating When Your Company Is Under Siege: Surviving Public Crisis*. Lexington Books, 1987.

Quirke, Bill. *Communicating Corporate Change: A Practical Guide to Communication and Corporate Strategy.* McGraw-Hill, 1996.

Ries, Al and Jack Trout. *Positioning: The Battle for Your Mind.* McGraw-Hill Professional Publishing, 2000.

Rossman, Marlene L. *Multicultural Marketing: Selling to be Diverse America.* AMACOM, 1994.

Sevier, Robert A. *Integrated Marketing for Colleges, Universities and Schools.* Council for Advancement and Support of Education, 1998.

Sevier, Robert A. *Strategic Planning in Higher Education: Theory and Practice.* Council for Advancement and Support of Education, 2000.

Sevier, Robert A. *Thinking Outside the Box: Think Strategically. Act Audaciously. Communicate Aggressively.* Strategy Publishing, Inc., 2001.

Sevier, Robert A. and Robert E. Johnson. *Integrated Marketing Communication: A Practical Guide to Developing Comprehensive Communication Strategies.* Council for Advancement and Support of Education, 1999

Tjosvold, Dean and Mary M. Tjosvold. *The Emerging Leader: Ways to a Stronger Team.* Lexington Books, 1993.

About the Author

Larry D. Lauer is vice chancellor for marketing and communication at Texas Christian University (TCU) in Fort Worth, TX. He is chairman of the TCU Marketing Advisory Board and holds the faculty rank of assistant professor of corporate and marketing communication.

Larry was executive director of The Commission on the Future of TCU, the University's major strategic planning initiative. He was the founding chairman of the Council for Advancement and Support of Education (CASE) advanced Seminar on Integrated Marketing in Higher Education, and has been a faculty member and chair of the CASE Summer Institute on Communications and Marketing at Duke University. He has worked with more than 25 campuses on integrated marketing initiatives in the United States, Canada, South America, South Africa, and the United Kingdom and has been a presenter at numerous regional, national, and international conferences.

He is the author of *Communication Power* (Aspen Publishers, 1997) and of more than 25 journal articles and book chapters on institutional marketing and communications. He has written articles on integrated marketing and planning for CASE *Currents* and *The CASE International Journal of Advancement*, and he has edited the first-ever section on marketing in the recently published third edition of CASE's *Handbook of Institutional Advancement*.

Index